RECOVERING FROM DIVORCE

RECOVERING FROM DIVORCE

A Practical Guide

Christopher Compston

HODDER AND STOUGHTON
LONDON   SYDNEY   AUCKLAND

British Library Cataloguing in Publication Data

A catalogue record for this book is
available from the British Library

ISBN 0-340-58630-3

Published by Hodder and Stoughton, a division of Hodder and Stoughton
Ltd, Mill Road, Dunton Green, Sevenoaks, Kent TN13 2YA. Editorial
Office: 47 Bedford Square, London WC1B 3DP.

Photoset by Rowland Phototypesetting Ltd, Bury St Edmunds, Suffolk

Printed in Great Britain by Cox and Wyman Ltd, Reading, Berks.

To Caroline

Contents

Acknowledgments

In a sense I have been writing this book for forty years, from 1953 to 1993. Year in, year out, I have been helped and encouraged by my family and friends. They are far too numerous to mention individually.

However, I must thank my mother, a most constant friend and support, and my wife, Caroline, loving and loyal – and my five children who, without doubt, are the best antidote to judicial pomposity!

This book developed from seminars which we lead at Holy Trinity, Brompton. I owe the staff, the fellowship and friends there an incalculable debt.

This book was typed by Cressida Inglis-Jones (and amended by Ali Groves). The draft was read and most usefully criticised by John and Diana Collins, Sandy and Annette Millar, Henrietta Usherwood and my wife.

I am very grateful to all of them and to many others, not least Rosemary Korbel and Christopher Perkins (the mainstays of the divorce recovery seminars), Ginny Cox, Nigel and Ursula Inglis-Jones and Janie Archbutt.

Introduction

In court, after all the evidence has been heard, the advocates make their speeches. Sometimes, the judge interrupts them asking, 'What is your authority for that proposition, Mr *Rumpole*?' 'Why should I prefer that piece of evidence or follow that case, or apply that act of Parliament?'

You may well ask, 'What is my authority for writing this book.'

My answer is threefold. First, in my own life, I have twice been through divorce. Second, for more than twenty-eight years, both as advocate and judge, I have been involved in hundreds of divorces. Third, in 1980, in the middle of my own divorce, I became a committed Christian, the turning point of my life.

Beginning with my own experiences: I was twelve when my parents divorced and I can vividly remember the unhappiness of that time, not least my father's absence, my mother's many difficulties and the constant lack of money. Forty years later, these wounds have now healed almost invisibly and I enjoy a good relationship with both my parents but some scar tissue remains.

There is nothing unique in my memories. A most able and sophisticated barrister was interviewed in the *Evening Standard*, July 4th, 1991: 'Rich and glamorous, heir to a baronetcy, married to a beautiful former model, living in an exquisite country house open to the public.' He had this to say about his parents' separation when he was twelve and their divorce when he was seventeen: 'I can't say that I look upon those five years with anything but wretchedness. The impact of their leading separate lives was something which I can never forget. Today, I think of divorce as being something I could not contemplate, not just because of the anguish and misery which it would cause me and my wife but because of the sense of despair it gives a child. You can't understand why these two people you love, whom you always regarded as the bedrock of your childhood, cannot love each other or at least live in the same house. Divorce causes utter misery all round.'

When I was twenty-eight I married a delightful girl. Apart from the death of our first son after thirty-six hours, we were, so far as I was aware, very happily married for ten years, with two splendid children. Then the marriage went on the rocks, ending in divorce. The painful misery of this time is unforgettable.

My professional background is more easily covered although I should stress that the views in this book are personal and not official. I was a barrister for over twenty years and, as such, handled many divorce cases, none of them glamorous or famous but all of them sad. Before I had my own troubles, while I could accept this sadness intellectually, it did not impinge on me emotionally at all. In any one month, I met at least twenty people involved in divorce. Usually their cases were 'undefended', both sides agreeing to end the marriage, usually tying up the children and the finances later. These cases meant that for about fifteen minutes I was intimately involved with somebody else's private life. No details were spared. Adultery, drunkenness, violence and the like were commonplace. In addition, there were the contested cases where husband and wife were fighting over money or their children. These cases sometimes took several days, and both in and out of court you got to know the inner workings of their marriage. As a judge for over seven years, I have found the experience is the same save that instead of hitting the matrimonial ball as hard as one could over the net, I am now an umpire. I have found this overall view to be very valuable.

As a corollary to my professional experience, over the last ten years, my present wife and I have counselled people who are contemplating or going through a divorce. 'Counselling' sounds pompous; often it merely means listening. *Over the last few years we have run divorce recovery seminars at our church.* (Details appear at the end of this book.)

Thus both personally and professionally, I have some experience of divorce and, although we are all unique, certain patterns of behaviour and misbehaviour emerge.

My third justification lies in my becoming a committed Christian in 1980 while going through the trauma of my own divorce. At the time, this could be called a crisis conversion. I was in trouble and, as cynical friends pointed out, found Christ as a crutch. Although I was indeed in great difficulty at the time, I can only add that, now that the crisis has passed, my Christian commitment remains, and whether you become a Christian through a crisis or less dramatically, it makes little odds in the end. The point is that you have made a commitment. What does this mean and what relevance has it to this book?

I realised in 1980 that, with my life in ruins, part of the blame lay at my door. With the shrewd but loving help of friends, I began to realise that the answer lay in Christ. I had to do three things. I had to repent of my sins (which were many). I then received Christ's forgiveness which was immediately given and immensely comforting. Thereafter, I had to rely on him. Repent, Receive, Rely. The jargon doesn't matter much and others may explain their conversion differently but, essentially, in writing as a committed Christian I fully believe God is all powerful and that the Bible is his inspired word.

And how is this relevant to this book? Here is the answer: if you become a Christian fully accepting Christ, the Holy Spirit – the third person of the Trinity – will guide and help you. Life will still have its problems but if you ask him, the Holy Spirit will be there to assist you with them. He makes an immeasurable, invaluable difference and is the golden thread running through this book.

If you are not a believer, some aspects of this book may not appeal but the points are still worth considering, so give them a chance. Many of them are plain common sense. Had I known them at the time, I know I would have recovered from my divorce more quickly.

A few general points may help you to get the best out of this book.

- – all Bible references are RSV (Revised Standard Version). I would suggest using whatever Bible you find most comfortable. A Bible with an index is always helpful. Write on it, mark it, underline it. Use it as a textbook.
- – in theory, the former concepts of 'innocent party' and 'guilty party' have gone, but in reality, there is usually one who actually delivers the final blow, by continuing the adultery, the drinking, the violence, or the like. In this book, by way of shorthand, I refer to the person who is on the receiving end, who doesn't want the divorce, as the 'victim' but I should stress that this is merely shorthand. In any marriage breakdown, both people are to some extent to blame. In a sense, both parties are victims (though the 'winner' may not appreciate it as yet). Save in the rarest of cases, children are always victims.
- – a few divorces are so difficult and the parties so intractable that even Solomon would have taken a second opinion, but these are rare. So beware of the cry, 'No one has suffered as much as I have.' Most of us have, I assure you, but we survived and so will you. This book is intended to support and encourage you. Remember God loves you, whatever you have done, and God, in the person of Jesus Christ, knows all about suffering.

• – finally, what do I mean by helpers? Help can range from the timely cup of tea or glass of beer to in-depth counselling by professionals. It all depends upon circumstances. In our experience, both at Holy Trinity, Brompton, and elsewhere, many people who help in this ministry have themselves suffered from divorce. This is hardly surprising since only those who have gone through it can fully appreciate the hell of it. Despite this, we have been immeasurably helped by many others, including the unmarried, the widowed and the happily married. The most surprising people have turned out to have the right touch. What is more, most of us are surely both victim and helper at the same time. As ever in the Christian life, I find that the more I help, or try to help, the more I receive in return.

A word about anecdotes. Although I have altered the details to safeguard privacy, I can vouch for the essential accuracy of all of them. Do such stories help? I am sure that they do and I freely confess that I often recall the stories told in sermons while I forget the theology almost as soon as I hear it. I take comfort from a well-known evangelist who recently told me that 85 per cent of the Bible is narrative and a mere 15 per cent theological.

Practical details are discussed in the final chapter. Essentially, this is a lay ministry but, within a church, it can only really be effective if it is carried out under the wing and with the blessing of the clergy and church leadership. I hope that ministers will read and endorse this book even if they leave much of the pastoral care to trusted lay helpers. In our church, we have been greatly helped and encouraged by the vicar and other church leaders who have left the daily details to us, always being available when required.

So may I end with a challenge to the Church. Many people feel that theologians only answer questions which people never ask. Many a time, out of duty, I have turned to the church section of a newspaper only to be so bored or confused that I give up after the first paragraph. What is more, so many of our established church leaders seem intent on debating the modern equivalent of the medieval puzzle as to how many angels you can get on a pinhead. All this is light years away from the grotty pain of divorce, inexorably claiming victims every minute of the day.

What can the Church do about this? It must face up to the reality that divorce, like AIDS, is not going to go away. Both scourges originate from sin but although God tells us to hate the sin, he equally tells us to love the sinner. For far too long the Church has viewed the divorced as second-class citizens even when they are or have become full members of the Church.

The Church's challenge lies in Isaiah 61:1:

> The Spirit of the Lord God is upon me,
>   because the Lord has anointed me
> to bring good tidings to the afflicted;
>   he has sent me to bind up the broken-hearted,
> to proclaim liberty to the captives,
>   and the opening of the prison to those
>   who are bound.

MARRIAGE

1 The Priorities in Marriage

In Britain, three million people will experience a broken marriage in the 1990s. One in five children can expect their parents to divorce before they reach the age of sixteen. One in seven families with dependent children have just one parent. These statistics are now so well known that there is a danger that their significance may well be lost. Let's put it like this: you are one of three brothers, one of you will be divorced. You have three children, one of them will be divorced. You glance around the pub, the office, the church and realise that every third couple will be divorced. Possibly you will, however unwillingly.

Sadly, being Christian is no proof against divorce. Likewise, being Christian is no guarantee of a happy marriage. For example, John Wesley, the founder of Methodism, was not happily married.

Some years ago, a family therapist invited some bishops and their wives to attend family therapy so that they would be better informed. Even he was surprised at the tensions unearthed in their marriages. I dare say they were surprised too!

This being so, I make no apologies for starting this book by majoring on marriage, its priorities and its enemies, for two good reasons. First, it would be wholly wrong for a committed Christian to write about divorce without first supporting marriage. Prevention is better than cure. All our marriages can be improved; far better to mend and improve than pick up the pieces after irretrievable breakdown. Divorce should be the last resort, not an easy first choice.

Lady Fisher, the stalwart wife of Lord Fisher, former Archbishop of Canterbury, was once asked about divorce. 'Divorce,' she snorted, 'divorce, never! But murder, often.'

Second, just as history tends to repeat itself so do our personal histories. Our personalities can make or mar us and within our marriage they are sorely tested. In many ways, it is so much easier to be good on your own. The single often have more money, more time, more space and, above all, more sleep! Therefore, if your marriage has failed or is failing – there is a possibility that the same strains may arise in your next relationship. Statistically, second marriages have a less than 30 per cent chance of surviving five years or more whereas third marriages have a less than 15 per cent chance. Hollywood abounds in colourful if pathetic examples. King Henry VIII had six wives – would you have gone to him for marriage guidance?

If we begin to know ourselves and discover what went wrong before, it is less likely to occur again. Looking at our past, therefore, may well make our present and future more secure. So, even if you are divorced or your marriage seems hopelessly on the rocks, read the next chapters: they are relevant. In fact, this book should be read as a whole, with underlying themes running right through.

Why marriage?

Marriage is ordained by God. In Genesis 2:24 we read, 'Therefore a man leaves his father and his mother and cleaves to his wife, and they become one flesh.' God established marriage for our welfare, our well-being. It was designed for the increase of the human race (Gen. 1:28, 'Be fruitful and multiply'). It was designed for our personal fulfilment (Gen. 2:18, 'It is not good that the man should be alone'). Therefore, in the words of Hebrews 13:4, 'Let marriage be held in honour among all.' Marriage is not a mere contract, a deal, to be broken at will or whim.

From marriage stems the family and, whatever your religious beliefs, you will probably agree that the family is the building-block of society. Destroy the family and you will have gone a very long way to undermining and ultimately destroying society. Those of us with large extended families, of all ages, know how valuable such families are. Though admittedly families can be difficult, those who run away from them are often running away from themselves.

Nowadays the family is under attack on all sides. The result is increased divorce, increased one-parent families, increased illegitimacy and increased loneliness, especially in old age. We can see this all around. The children coming from these backgrounds may be less well equipped for later life by their lopsided start. However hard their single parents try, they have an agonisingly difficult job. Children get their first sense of values from their parents so they are considerably disadvantaged if raised by only one. We should strive to rebuild marriages and families both for our own sakes and for society's.

Priorities

The problem is how to do it. We should start with getting our priorities right. First, love God, then our husband or wife, then our children, then our work and our hobbies.

Above all, love God. As Jesus told us in Matthew 22:37–8, 'You shall love the Lord your God with all your heart, and with all your soul, and with all your mind. This is the first and great commandment.' If we do so, or try to do so, we find that so many of our problems disappear or fall into more manageable perspective.

Preachers at weddings, referring to the bride and groom, give the most useful picture of a triangle. God is at the top and the apex of the triangle has the bridegroom on the bottom left and the bride on the bottom right. The preacher tells the bride and groom to get close to God and thus closer to each other.

Our next priority is to love our husband or wife, not our parents, not our children, not our friends. On marriage, the human relationship of child/parent is replaced by another: that of husband/wife. Sometimes this doesn't happen, either because the parents don't leave the children alone or the children run to the parents.

On the other hand, many parents love their children more than each other. Considering how attractive young children are and how tired and tetchy we parents can sometimes be, this is understandable. 'We have given up everything for the kids' – and the result? Often, the children either become smothered by such obsessive love that they grow up stunted and inadequate, or they just rebel. Children must be allowed to flee the nest although our homes should always be open to them.

Finally work: this includes good works just as much as earning your living. When I became a Christian I was separated from my first wife and children and discovered that it was quite possible to be involved in Christian activities every day of the week.

I am grateful to my old barristers' clerk, Ian Evans, now an ordained baptist minister, for saying, 'Whether it's the pub or the church, to your children you are just not there.' Wise words which I hope he now follows. Save on rare occasion or in dire emergency, your family should come before good works.

What about normal work? Most people, with rising expenses in these difficult times, have to work very hard to earn their living and, even then, may fail to make ends meet. Their wives may have to go out to work with all the attendant difficulties of getting help with the children either inside or outside the home. This puts a great strain on the marriage and on the children.

A recent Gallup poll analysed in spring 1992, showed

that 90 per cent of mothers in paid employment have difficulty combining their roles. They face practical and emotional problems.

Without being glib, you may well have to consider or reconsider what really matters in life. Is it promotion or is it Peter? Is it the Volvo or is it Veronica? Is it France or is it Francis? Assuredly, we can't take our money or our fame with us when we die. Here and now, please read 1 Timothy 6:6–10 and if you have a Bible underline the verses.

> There is great gain in godliness with contentment; for we brought nothing into the world, and we cannot take anything out of the world; but if we have food and clothing, with these we shall be content. But those who desire to be rich fall into temptation, into a snare, into many senseless and hurtful desires that plunge men into ruin and destruction. For the love of money is the root of all evil; it is through this craving that some have wandered away from the faith and pierced their hearts with many pangs.

When the American multimillionaire Rockefeller died, someone asked, 'What did he leave?', only to be given the chilling reply, 'He left everything.' Remember Cardinal Newman's prayer, 'Teach me Lord, frequently and attentively to consider this truth: that if I gain the whole world and lose thee, in the end I have lost everything: whereas if I lose the world and gain thee, in the end I have lost nothing.'

To give quality time to your wife and children may mean that you have to turn down certain offers, forgo certain opportunities, give up certain hobbies. Easier said than done, but if your job takes you constantly away from home, you may have to consider changing your job. Fine advice in the middle of a recession but the pressures on your health and your family's happiness may justify change.

Furthermore, if you stand firm, some compromise may well be reached. The director of a well-known bank in London insisted on being home in time to bath and read to his four young children. He is still a director, still has a delightful wife and the bank still prospers. Again, we know a competent businessman who for the last twenty-three years has worked only four days a week. Admittedly, this is not easy to achieve, but some adjustment may be possible. The converse is sad. Some years ago, I met the wife of a most successful man. She, her clothes and her jewellery were beautiful and she lived in one of the most expensive parts of London. Yet, after two glasses of wine, what bitterness. 'You can keep all this,' she said. 'I never see him – he never sees the children, so what's it all about?' What indeed!

A word about hobbies. Some hobbies are more wholesome than others, but the golf widow is just as abandoned as the pub widow. We may have to tailor our hobbies to the justified needs of our wife and children.

Incidentally, please don't think that I am advocating failure in the world. When Jesus said in John 10:10, 'I came that they may have life, and have it abundantly' he meant that Christians should have richly fulfilled lives. I often quote that Heineken advertisement, 'Reaching the parts that others can't reach' to show that, since becoming a Christian, my life has become increasingly more fulfilling, more exciting, more fun than I could ever have imagined possible. The Christian life is not grey dullness or mediocrity but it may not entail great riches or great public success. Undoubtedly we should do our very best in our jobs. We should play our part in the world outside the Church, always rendering Caesar his due. Our commission is to evangelise the world: Matthew 28:19, 'Go therefore and make disciples of all nations,' and we won't succeed in this if we never move outside the Christian ghetto.

Other relationships

Finally, we should remember other family relationships, with our parents, our brothers and sisters and other family members, as well as friends. The fifth commandment, in Exodus 20:12, says, 'Honour your father and your mother, that your days may be long in the land which the Lord your God gives you.' We should strive to be in a right relationship with God our Father and with our own parents.

This may not be easy; there may be many fences to mend. Our parents may have let us down; we may have let them down. If parents, we know how difficult parenting is. All the more reason for us to view our own parents' apparent failures with sympathetic understanding. God tells us to honour them, so honour them we must. In fact, whatever our ages, they have much to teach us. The better our relationship with our parents, the better our relationship with our married partner and with our own children. If one relationship is out of true, this must have a knock-on effect on the other. To make a perfect square, all four corners have to be at right angles. Particularly in the Western world, we have lost the respect due to age; society is continuing to pay a heavy price for this folly.

At the same time, we should try and be in good relationship with our brothers and sisters and wider family. They are our generation and likely to outlive our parents and, in many ways, to be more available when our children have flown the nest. I often think of two sisters, now well in their eighties, whose friendship, through thick and thin, has undoubtedly enriched their lives and still does. They contrast with two sisters of similar age whose relationship, blighted by problems which began before the First World War, has been considerably less happy. What a pity.

You cannot expect total fulfilment in one relationship if other relationships are less than God requires.

One final word. I recently met a woman who had fifty-six first cousins, yet there are some with no family at all. Christians should always remember that we are all God's children. We are all brothers and sisters and our heart and home should be especially open to the lonely. We should 'adopt' a granny or aunt or sister. If we do, it will be a two-way traffic. We will get as much as we give.

2   The Enemies of Marriage

Katharine Whitehorn, the newspaper columnist, once wrote that we should see our marriages more as fires that might need stoking rather than flames that have blown out. Wise and witty. We maintain our cars, surely we should do the same with our marriages? If only we could give our marriages an MOT test every year. With God's help, we can do so.

A picture may help you. View your marriage as a house. Houses need maintenance. When we marry, our marriage house is new. Over the years, our marriage house, almost imperceptibly, settles down. The odd tile comes off. The paint gets a little chipped. The carpet gets worn. God willing, children come. Unless we are very careful, our marriage house deteriorates and can, of course, deteriorate so badly that it has to be demolished.

As a keen gardener, I prefer the picture of a garden. If you fail to take care of your garden, it soon gets out of control. For some months, I neglected my allotment. What happened? It became invaded with nettles, grass and bindweed. It took hours and hours of happy labour, ably assisted by our four-year-old son, Rupert, to get it back into good shape. Had we maintained it regularly, such heroic efforts would not have been needed.

Time

One of the greatest enemies of marriage is time. How to find time for marriage, with all the other pressing demands, is very difficult indeed. Not least when so many of these demands are 'good' demands. Our parents, our children, our friends, the Church and the needy, all have legitimate claims upon us. When we have dealt with them and are looking forward to peace and quiet alone, with our wife, what happens? So often, a child wakes, a friend telephones, a neighbour calls – yet another claim is made upon our time and the chance of quality time alone, however short, has passed. The spell of intimacy is broken and on we rush. It has been well put, 'The devil is not in a hurry, the devil is hurry.'

Faced with these challenges, a few obvious remedies come to mind. Planning helps. We plan our public life; why not plan our private life? The Americans are particularly good at this although some of their charts are a little daunting. We can plan, or at least attempt to plan, so that we have some time for each other without interruption. This can be done daily, weekly, monthly, annually. In my first marriage we didn't appreciate let alone tackle this problem at all, so what follows is the wisdom of hindsight.

Try to have a few minutes alone with each other every day, both in the morning and in the evening.

A week can be better organised. My wife always keeps our diary ever since the occasion when we discovered that at 7 p.m. we had double booked to see different friends! Now, we try to keep an evening a week free for our-selves.

Put a sticker in the diary meaning at home alone, so that you can truthfully say, 'I am sorry, we are engaged that night.' A treat together once a month helps. This need not be expensive – it could be a drink in the park. The details are down to you. The principle is the point. Time for each other alone. Finally, each year, some days away are invaluable. As explained later, friends can help here.

Fun is essential. It is hard being grown up all the time. Just unwinding, temporarily shedding one's responsibilities, is essential for health and happiness. Tension can build up remorselessly unless we consciously learn to relax.

Moreover, we must take an overall view of our general situation if we are to make the best use of our time, always remembering that the good is the enemy of the best. In other words, before either of you take on any additional activity, do pray about it, discuss it and agree it first. Christians are particularly prone to taking on too many 'good' activities with the result that, often, these activities are not very well done, they themselves get tired and burnt out and their home life suffers. We have to learn to say no.

A few years ago, I stupidly broke this rule by becoming treasurer to a local old people's home. It was only once a week, the home was just across the road and the old people were delightful. Yet we had too much to do anyway; I should have said no. After a few months, I dreaded the weekly visit from the warden. 'Old Annie wants to pay half cash half cheque,' 'old Gertrude thinks you have stolen her rent,' and 'old Alan's failing. Do you think he should go to another home?' This small duty nearly broke the camel's back. I should never have accepted. So, look at any commitment with great care. Have you the time, the skill, the energy? Is this what God wants you to do? If you follow the life of Jesus, it is quite clear that he always did what his Father told him to do when, in every village and town, there must have been people who needed his loving attention. Notwithstanding, he moved on. He had more important things to do.

Lack of Communication

A second enemy of marriage is lack of communication. Some people may never have really communicated. At first they were so 'in love' that they never realised they really had very little in common. Others, when first married, communicated very well, sharing feelings all the time until, with increasing responsibilities, they communicated less and less. One train on one track became two trains on parallel tracks until the tracks began to diverge. No longer one flesh but two lonely people.

Communication entails emotional communication of feelings, not mere thoughts. In short, both must say, 'What are my *feelings* about this or that?' WAMFA. What are my *feelings* about . . . the way you drive, the way you look, the way you speak to me, the way you speak to the children? A very experienced marriage review team ask couples to face such questions alone and then together. Hard going but worth doing. We understand with our mind. We *feel* with our heart.

People who are not prepared to communicate, are the ultimate losers. In marriage, if you can't communicate, you are in deep trouble.

Ken Crispin, an Australian lawyer, has written a most useful book, *Divorce – The Forgivable Sin?*, in which he details how a marriage can deteriorate. The first stage is the stage of erosion. During this there is a tendency to avoid confrontation, to avoid certain taboo topics. The result is the gradual but remorseless erosion of intimacy between man and wife. If you are at this stage it is as well to face it bravely and, if Christian, pray about it and get others, suitably chosen, to pray for you. If you don't, the stage of detachment will follow. By now, the walls between man and wife are well and truly up. There may be no open hostility between them. In fact, in many ways, life may be easier during this stage than during the first more painful stage of erosion. The reason is that, frankly, the people don't really care about each other at all. They are no longer one flesh but two separate beings, ripe for picking off by others. Once this stage is reached, the marriage is in very great danger.

'A stitch in time saves nine.' If there is a problem in your marriage, tackle it early rather than late. Going back to the picture of the house, suppose you saw an ominous patch of fungus underneath the sink, presumably you would take action at once. Dry rot can spread like wildfire; it can destroy the house. Likewise, in your marriage, if there is a problem face it and face your partner with it as boldly and as lovingly as you can before it gets out of control. If I had done so in my first marriage, I wonder whether it might have been saved. As it was, I buried my head in the sand hoping the problem would go away.

However painful, tackle the problem soon before it is too late. Christians are often in difficulties here, hiding their problems out of pride. We may be prepared to admit to God that we have problems, but we are not prepared to admit them to each other. We certainly wouldn't admit them to fellow Christians. Why is it that, in certain churches, we always have to say that life is fine and dandy when it isn't? This is wholly wrong. In the Christian family, subject to certain safeguards, all of us should be able to admit that we are going through a rough time. The congregation, triumphantly singing the 'Hallelujah Chorus', should always be sensitively aware of those temporarily unable to join in.

A corollary to this is found in Ephesians 4:26, 'Do not let the sun go down on your anger.' Try to say sorry, to forgive as soon as possible, and always by the time you go to sleep at night. This is hard, gritted teeth and all that, but, ideally, over every double bed should be emblazoned, 'Do not let the sun go down on your anger.'

Keep short accounts with God and likewise with your marriage partner. Don't let small tensions accumulate. Try and start every day at square one.

Other people

A third enemy is other people. Over the last ten years, I have twice counselled ordained ministers whose marriages were potentially in danger from another woman. I should stress that neither of them had any connection whatsoever with my present church.

No adultery took place. The temptation faced, the temptation was overcome. I only mention these two incidents because they made me realise how even the most stalwart Christians are prone to attack. Many Christian circles are not good at handling these crises or potential situations. I recall a case I had in the Crown Court. A minister, admirable in so many ways, was lonely and committed a comparatively minor offence against a young teenager. He was sent to prison. In conference, he well described his dilemma. Realising that he might well succumb to temptation, he also realised that there was no one, literally no one, to whom he could turn. His family loved him but would have been shocked beyond words. Like a captain on a ship, he could not discuss such intimate problems with the officers below him. As for his fellow ministers, he feared to tell them. I have no doubt at all that, helped in time, these incidents would never have occurred.

Caustic Charlie and drunken Dave may be as much of a danger as beautiful Belinda or handsome Harry. Aren't we all aware of amusing and attractive people, good fun but essentially unwholesome, even dangerous? They are insidiously tempting. Far better to avoid temptation in the first place than flirt with it. In short, don't give any of them a foot in the door. This advice applies to individuals or groups: quite calmly, we have to say, 'I am not going to mix with that lot.' If we want to help them and tell them about our faith, we should do so from a safe position, fortified by prayer. Again, tackle this early. Please note: this is not because we are so holy. It is because we are so unholy. In other words, we try to avoid temptation because we know how easy it is to fall.

Always remember that temptation is not a sin. Many, myself included, when tempted have felt guilty of sin. The sin lies not in temptation but in feeding the temptation and giving way to it. Give the devil an inch and he will take a mile. Try and avoid taking the first steps. If you are an alcoholic don't walk home via the pub or the off-licence and certainly don't take a job in a pub! Remember 1 Corinthians 10:13, 'No temptation has overtaken you that is not common to man. God is faithful, and he will not let you be tempted beyond your strength, but with the temptation will also provide the way of escape, that you may be able to endure it.' Jesus was tempted.

Serious marriage problems

This list is not exhaustive but would include persistent unfaithfulness, alcoholism, drugs, violence, homosexuality. In a sense, any misbehaviour should be taken seriously. A sin is always a sin. However, there are major problems which we find too hard to handle alone or even with the help of a small circle of friends. These problems cannot properly be tackled here but certain guidelines may assist.

First, try to decide whether the problem is personal or stems from the relationship. Is there an underlying problem quite apart from marriage? Of course, the marriage may have caused it to surface and you cannot separate the individual and the marriage, but try to be objective. Has he always had a drink problem? Has she always been paranoid? If the answer is yes this will help you enormously. You won't feel burdened by guilt that you may have caused it and you will be better able to take proper professional advice.

Charles II, the Merry Monarch, died in 1685. He was habitually unfaithful to his long-suffering queen; his illegitimate children are the ancestors of some of the present English aristocracy. His faithful wife, loving him to the end, should not have felt much to blame, such was the carnal nature of her husband.

Second, decide whether the problem is major or minor. Was this a one-off incident which can be handled within the marriage or was it a symptom for something far more serious, requiring professional help? It is all a matter of degree. If he returns home drunk from the office party probably you can handle it. If he pours whisky on his breakfast cornflakes, probably you can't.

Third, take the best professional advice and stick to it.

Having called in the experts try and co-operate with them. If your doctor told you to lose weight otherwise you would have a heart attack, you would probably follow his advice. Likewise, if a competent adviser suggests a course of action, follow the advice. Serious problems warrant serious effort.

Finally, tell only a small circle of confidential friends and don't let them change your course of action, unless for very good reason. For instance: your husband is being unfaithful, your experienced adviser advises you to play hard to get; your best friend says, 'Oh no, fall into his arms whenever he comes home.' I don't know who is right (though I would put my money on the adviser) but I do know that, in any battle, you should have a consistent battle plan with one general in charge. Time and time again, people get advice from A, then B, and then C and wonder why they end up in a muddle. In fact, there is no right answer to their problem. A's battle strategy has good points, so has B's and so has C's. What is clear is that you cannot try all three at once.

Furthermore, even in these difficult situations, painful as they are, you and your friends should be as discreet as possible. He may be violent. She may be unfaithful. However, the children still love their parents; you may be reconciled and, to harm their public reputation out of temporary spite could well ruin them, with serious consequences for you and your children.

3 Marriage Takes Commitment

Many years ago, I was sitting in my garden, talking to an older married woman. She seemed old to me. In fact, she was probably forty-nine! I will always remember her words: 'Christopher, if only you younger people knew some of the muddles and messes we got into years ago, you wouldn't be nearly so worried.' She then discussed some of our staid old neighbours and how different their lives had been twenty years before. Her clear message was persevere. Life isn't always a bed of roses and, from time to time, marriage is very hard work.

Lack of time, lack of communication, and other people are enemies of marriage; but *the* enemy is lack of commitment. Unless you are really committed to your marriage, when problems arise, as they undoubtedly will, you may very well fail. In the end, it often comes down to staying-power, that good old-fashioned word 'guts', the guts to continue fighting for your marriage even when the going is very rough indeed. Nowadays, in these days of instant results and instant gratification, people often give up on their marriage without really trying.

You can read as many books as you like. You can go to as many doctors and therapists as you like, you can talk endlessly with your family and friends, you can even pray or convince yourself that you are praying but, if you are not deeply committed to your marriage, these supports will be of little avail.

Let me give some cogent examples. At the same time that my first marriage was in difficulties, so were four other marriages, with one partner having an affair on the side. All of us had young children. However, these four couples wanted their marriages to survive, partly for their own sakes and certainly for the sake of their children, and despite serious difficulties they worked at and through their problems. They were committed to their marriages and, fourteen years later, they are still married; they showed staying-power and it paid off.

Helen Lee, in her book *Christian Marriage* (Mowbrays, 1977, p. 159) puts it well: 'Solving people's marriage problems has more to do with the character of the people than the complexities of the situation.' St Paul is an unusual role model for marriage but let us compare his character with the complexities he had to meet. As we read in 2 Corinthians 11:24–7,

Five times I have received at the hands of the Jews the forty lashes less one. Three times I have been beaten with rods; once I was stoned. Three times I have been shipwrecked; a night and a day I have been adrift at sea; on frequent journeys, in danger from rivers, danger from robbers, danger from my own people, danger from Gentiles, danger in the city, danger in the wilderness, danger at sea, danger from false brethren; in toil and hardship, through many a sleepless night, in hunger and thirst, often without food, in cold and exposure.

Some complexities but what character!

Your marriage may be so difficult that separation, if not divorce, is inevitable. The point I wish to stress is that marriage requires hard work and that if you persevere you may well win through.

Furthermore, love is not dependent on feelings. Of course, feelings are very important but love must be made of sterner stuff. We may have to use our will, almost going on automatic pilot, when our feelings are at a low ebb. Hollywood and the like have done immeasurable harm in spreading the myth that love is mere candyfloss and that when the candyfloss goes then off you go too. It is nonsense.

One final point. Let's go back to our picture of the marriage house or garden. If we were told that we could not move from either our house or our garden what would we do? As I write this, in these difficult days of recession, the picture is probably rather more realistic than it was some years ago. God tells us that marriage is permanent. Surely, if we know that we can't move house, we do our level best to live in it, making all necessary adaptations and alterations. If we can't move our garden, we will have to adapt our planting to the soil and site. We may well like rhododendrons but if they won't grow in our soil then we will have to find alternatives. Surely, faced with this challenge, most of us can make an excellent job of it even if originally it was not quite what we had in mind. So persevere.

Making it better

So, if married, how can we help make our marriage better? If divorced, how could we have made our marriage work? The point here being not a bitter post-mortem but a frank evaluation of the past so that we can have happy lives now and in the future.

This book is not primarily concerned with marriage. Others, with considerably more authority than I (after all they haven't failed!) have both written and spoken wisely and well. However, the following guidelines may assist.

Books
Even the most indifferent cook has some cookery books on the kitchen shelf. Others have whole libraries, not that they are necessarily the best cooks! How many of us have even onc book on marriage?

I have recommended some books at the end. I have read them all. Like the curate's egg, they are good in parts. You may well find it useful to read some of them and if you do so, you will clearly see how I have used some of their ideas and images.

Two slight words of caution. First, if your marriage is in difficulties, I advise reading such books discreetly. To sit up in bed reading *How To Make Your Husband/Wife Perfect* is hardly tactful. Once you have mastered and digested the contents then share them by all means and, if the time is right, share the book as well.

Second, if you are going to lend a book, not only should you have read it but try to pick the right book. If your husband is in the army and has just come back from a commando course, he may well not get excited about a book with a bunch of daffodils on the cover. A life of Leonard Cheshire, founder of the Cheshire Homes, who won the Victoria Cross in the Second World War, may be a better bet. By the same token, a highly-strung woman may well find an earthy Christian sex manual more than she can cope with at such a time.

Videos and tapes
The same principles apply. It is hard to discuss a book in a group unless everyone has read it. Group-listening to tapes can be a little tedious unless the tape is particularly good. Videos, on the other hand, are excellent for group discussion and, if tactfully handled, may well lead to useful conversations, not least between you and your husband or wife privately afterwards.

Seminars
There are some excellent public seminars. I have not specifically recommended any because the details and the leaders change but your church or a large well-established local church should be able to supply details. Ideally, they should be led by couples who are realistic, amusing and down to earth, preferably having many responsibilities and their own children. Avoid those who preach at or down to you.

Alternatively after prayer and preparation, you might

consider having informal marriage seminars of your own, covering aspects of marriage and parenthood. These can be invaluable, not least because you know the parties concerned, both the speakers and the audience. They should be done well or not at all.

Marriage review weekends

There are very experienced couples who run such courses and are training others so to do. We have attended two, with considerable benefit, not that it was always easy having to face ourselves so intimately! Although these can be comparatively expensive, they are worth every penny and, if your means are tight, your church should be able to help. One of the great advantages is that you are in relaxed surroundings, without your children and with all your usual responsibilities suspended. Another advantage is that you may well find kindred spirits with whom you can share your problems. Very often, you are not likely to meet them again so, provided you know what you are doing, you can probably be more open and frank to them than you would to many in your own church.

And, finally and crucially, prayer.

Prayer

Again and again, we are told to pray. In Ephesians 6:18, 'Pray at all times in the Spirit, with all prayer and supplication.' In 1 Thessalonians 3:10, Paul talks of 'praying earnestly night and day' and, a few lines later, in 1 Thessalonians 5:17, tells the Thessalonians 'pray constantly'. So pray.

We should pray for our own marriage and for our own children as well as for other people. Every day, try to pray for your marriage, asking the Holy Spirit to join you in making it better.

Always pray for your children, even grown-up children. Every night we pray for God's protection upon our children and for their future life, praying for their marriages, their children and their children's children.

This last prayer may well seem 'over the top' but since the Old Testament teaches us that the effects of sin can be felt to the fourth generation, why shouldn't we pray for blessings for the fourth generation? Although we may not know it, how many of us have reason to be grateful for long-dead grandparents or great grandparents who prayed for us?

Postscript

This book is not primarily concerned with marriage, but those wishing to help marriage might consider the following points:

- In an emergency, anyone can help, but preferably build up an experienced marriage guidance/review team who pray and meet regularly.
- It is unwise to help the opposite sex alone. Christians are not immune from temptation.
- Two heads are often better than one. We men may well miss a clue which our wives pick up, and vice versa.
- Practical and financial help, especially in times of stress, may make the crucial difference. Small acts of kindness are often more valuable than the big gesture.
- Always encourage. 'Therefore encourage one another and build one another up' (1 Thess. 5:11).

DURING A DIVORCE

4 Can I Divorce? Should I Divorce?

This question can be asked in two ways. Legally, what is the position? Morally, what is the position? Sadly, the two do not always overlap.

The law

Legally, the answer is simple. Over the last decades, in Great Britain, it has become increasingly easier to obtain a divorce. Up-to-date statistics are not yet available but, by way of example, the rate of divorce in the UK doubled between 1971 and 1988. Each year the parents of around 150,000 children under sixteen are divorced. A 1990s study commissioned by Relate (formerly the Marriage Guidance Council) estimated that the cost to government of divorce and separation in 1987–8 was 1.3 billion pounds. Britain now has the highest divorce rate of all the Western European countries, a third higher than in France and six times higher than in Italy. It also has one of the highest rates of births outside marriage, almost 30 per cent.

Essentially, the courts have to be satisfied that the marriage is irretrievably broken down on certain specified grounds. These are adultery, unreasonable behaviour, desertion, being separated for two years with consent, and five years without consent. Any lawyer, library or Citizens Advice Bureau can tell you the details.

Remember, the law is not in the business of saving marriages. Once people pass through the solicitor's door, they very rarely turn back. As a barrister, I never saw a reconciliation. As a judge, I have only annulled one divorce because of a reconciliation. Suffice it to say that, save in the rarest of circumstances, if anyone wishes to obtain a divorce, in law they can. It is quite another question whether this is desirable. Many Christians feel that it is not.

Morally, the situation is far less clear. I am no theologian and if you have theological doubts or concerns you should raise them with your minister. Views vary considerably, not only from Christian denomination to Christian denomination but even within denominations. Thus, the vicar of B may well say, 'No problem,' whereas the vicar of East B, just down the road, may say, 'Over my dead body.' What is clear is that if you have doubts it is better to resolve them now rather than later. Guilt, like bitterness, can eat away at your health and happiness.

Here are some points for you to consider:

- First, remember marriage is not *a human invention* but *God's creation*. If we believe that God is Alpha and Omega, the beginning and the end, then anything which he created should be treated with considerable respect. We tamper with his laws at our peril.
- Second, in the Old Testament, there was some Mosaic provision for divorce as a temporary concession to human sin. But in Malachi 2:16 we read that God hates divorce.
- Third, in the New Testament Jesus endorsed the permanence of marriage and in Matthew 19:9 said, 'Whoever divorces his wife, except for unchastity (porneia) and marries another, commits adultery'.
- Fourth, St Paul with authoritative, apostolic instruction in 1 Corinthians 7:10–16 permitted divorce on the desertion of an unbelieving partner.
- Finally, divorce was permitted when both the marriage

and the divorce had been prior to salvation; as 2 Corinthians 5:17 triumphantly reminds us, after salvation, 'if anyone is in Christ, he is a new creation; the old has passed away, behold the new has come'.

The issue of divorce has exercised great thinkers over the centuries; I have neither the time nor the ability to go further into these matters, save to add that some Christians have found great comfort in the covenant principle. Ken Crispin, already mentioned, usefully summarises this principle as follows:

(a) If a marriage becomes intolerable to one party in the sense that the conduct of the other party is such that a proper marital relationship is no longer viable, then a Christian husband or wife may proceed to divorce, that is, proceed to sever the marital relationship. Even after actually leaving, however, any reasonable areas of reconciliation should be explored and it is only when it has become clear that no reconciliation can be achieved that the marriage should be regarded as at an end.

(b) Once that point has been reached, in Biblical terms, the couple is already divorced and may feel free to regularise the situation by proceeding to obtain a legal decree and to resolve any issues concerning the children of the marriage and any matrimonial property.

(c) To the extent that a person is at fault for the breakdown of the marriage, that person will need to seek forgiveness. No matter how responsible they are for the termination of that marriage, however, God will forgive and that person will be free to remarry and to start a new life.

Should I divorce?

Many of us divorce against our wishes so realistically we
are more concerned with those, either individuals or
couples, who are still contemplating whether to proceed
or not. Under God, only you can decide. You take the
decision, not your lawyers, though some lawyers tend to
forget this! The step is so important and so irrevocable
that, before taking it, it is as well to think very carefully
indeed, taking the wise advice of a few selected friends
and, if a Christian, remembering that prayer is essential.
When praying, thinking and discussing, the following
points should be borne well in mind. Frankly, in the cold
pages of a book, it is hard to do some of them justice.

Pain

Divorce is very painful. Usually it is most painful for the
victim, though even those pressing for a divorce will be surprised at their intermittent bouts of pain. From time to
time, when going through a divorce, the pain is almost overwhelming, it is so acute. At other times, the pain is dormant
but can strike without warning. Only those who have been
through it can fully understand. Two pictures may help.
Hans Christian Andersen retold the old legend of the mer-
maid who became human in order to capture the handsome
prince. Every step she took on land was as if a knife was
running through her body. Closer to home, when we were
in pain as children we ran to our parents' arms. As a husband or wife in pain we may run, only to remember while
running that it is he or she who is causing the pain.

As a divorce barrister, I accepted intellectually that the
parties were in pain. But only when it happened to me
did I begin to understand emotionally what the people
had been going through.

Some years back, after my present wife had had two
miscarriages, a sympathetic doctor's wife told us that even
her own husband had not appreciated the pain of miscar-

riage until she herself had one. Then, permanently, his attitude to his patients changed.

Indeed, even now, fifteen years later, I recall a man, as macho as they come, bursting into tears in conference at the sheer misery caused him by his wife's adultery. Not only are you in pain, but so are your family who so often tend to be ignored at this stage save as a sounding board or possible retreat. But what about them? Particularly as we get older, much of our life is bound up with the happiness of our children and grandchildren. Finally, and this can never be stressed enough, the pain caused to our children is incalculable. Even if they appear to be better off at the moment or 'not to be taking it too badly' in nearly every case they are harmed and these harmful effects can last a lifetime. Time and time again, we meet people, including old people, still not recovered from their parents' divorce. This can be passed on to their children in turn. Not surprisingly, if you have had poor role models as parents, you are less likely to be a good role model yourself. By the same token, child abusers have often themselves been abused as children.

Grief
Grief is different from pain though intimately bound up with it. If you divorce, you will be involved in a grief situation just as poignantly, perhaps even more so than being widowed. It takes a long time to recover from grief. Some people never do. Well into their seventies, even eighties, they are still recounting, as yesterday, the wrongs done them nearly fifty years ago.

Guilt
As Christians we know that we need not suffer from guilt because Jesus, by dying on the Cross, bore our sins and we are freed from their effect if we repent and believe in him. However, although many of us appreciate this we are riddled with guilt. If we have mainly caused the divorce we should quite rightly feel ashamed because we have

betrayed our marriage and betrayed our children. If we wish to be truly free of this guilt, we should repent and say sorry both to God and man, including our former husband or wife. Even if years have passed, you can still repent and, perhaps, write a letter saying how sorry you are to the people you have wronged. Even if you are the victim, you may still be riddled with guilt, feeling an almost intolerable sense of failure. Intellectually, you may realise that you are far from being all to blame and your loyal family and friends will repeatedly tell you so. But the fact remains that, emotionally, you just feel a failure all the time and in all spheres, not just your failed marriage. This is a very heavy burden which, as detailed later, can and must be overcome if you are going to regain your health and happiness. If you are contemplating divorce, face the fact that you will feel guilty even if essentially you are not to blame.

Anger

You will feel very angry, particularly if you are the victim. In a way, this anger is natural and healthy. It has a purpose. It may well be an important driving force for many people. The Bible tells us that God can be angry and all of us remember Jesus, full of justified anger, throwing the traders out of the temple. Anger, if handled well and ultimately overcome, can both refine and strengthen you. You will have to work through it. The point is that, at this stage, it is a very painful experience.

In May 1992 the world delighted, for a few hours, in the antics of Lady Moon, the estranged wife of the fifth baronet, Sir Peter Graham-Moon. As she put it, 'To relieve . . . intense hurt and frustration', she snipped the sleeves off her husband's Savile Row suits, daubed his BMW motorcar with paint and deposited his vintage wines on the village doorsteps, thereby causing damage of about £30,000. My first reaction was sympathetic. She had apparently had a raw deal and why not get her own back? My second reaction was a little more judicial. She committed various criminal offences, cost the family a good deal of money, and doubtless caused her sons considerable embarrassment. On balance, it was probably not very wise. Therefore, realise that you will be angry but, if you can, avoid letting anger harm either you or others. Do nothing irrevocable.

Loneliness

If you have been reasonably happily married you will be very lonely when divorced. Moreover, even the person who wanted the divorce will, at times, feel lonely if they have any residual conscience. Both of you can assuage some of this inner loneliness by outside activities but lonely you will undoubtedly be. One writer has talked of a 'deep and pervasive feeling of loneliness – the loneliness cuts like a knife. It twists and turns and the pain can be relentless and unbearable, both for the one who left and the one who remains.' Even with a new lover, you can still feel lonely.

Pausing there, let me introduce 'Frantic Fred' and 'Forlorn Freda'. They are both victims of loneliness. Fred spends all his waking moments doing things in a desperate effort to avoid facing his loneliness. Freda, equally tormented, does nothing at all, being almost drowned in depression. Both characters are to be pitied and, to some extent, you will be one or the other, sometimes both on the same day.

Incidentally, you may well find as I did that you will be willing to alter your value system, your general code of behaviour, because you rashly and wrongly think that such a change will bring you relief. You start to drink or smoke too much, mix with the wrong company, even sleep around. This may bring relief in the short run but in the long run, it will not.

Children

It is enough to say that your children will be hurt. 'Whoever causes one of these little ones who believe in me to sin, it would be better for him if a great millstone were hung round his neck and he were thrown into the sea' (Mark 9:42).

Divorce is always painful for children, *whatever their ages*. For many years, I believed that provided parents stuck together until the children left school then, all in all, 'it wasn't all that bad'. I now believe that most children are hurt, whatever their age, and hurt badly even if, being adult, they are able to disguise their hurt quite well. Furthermore, your children's loss of trust in you is inevitable where you have broken your marriage promises. Two-thirds of people involved in divorce have children.

Financial

Although divorce is legally easier, it cannot cut the cake into two cakes of equal size. Unless you are extremely rich divorce leads to financial problems, often very damaging financial problems. This is hardly surprising. Lawyers, estate agents, sometimes doctors and psychiatrists get involved and have to be paid. Usually the family home has to be sold and one parent with the children rehoused in inferior accommodation. If employed, your firm may be prepared to carry you for a while even if you do have days off but if you are self-employed you will just lose that day's income. By rule of thumb, I endorse a friend who said that his divorce set him back ten years in his profession. Thus, at forty-five and with many responsibilities, he had the status and income of a thirty-five-year-old having dropped so many rungs on the professional ladder. He could never regain those lost rungs. As an American put it, 'Financial life after divorce is the pits!'

Divorce is not a final solution

Finally, remember that unless yours is a short marriage, with no children, divorce is not a final solution. It is a solution of sorts in that, once divorced, you are free to remarry, but you may still have financial responsibilities towards your wife and you will undoubtedly have emotional and financial responsibilities towards your children.

These will not go away for many years. What is more, as your children grow up, you will have to face school functions and weddings and, when they have children, you will have to face christenings and parties and the like. Death is final: divorce is not. Divorce is not an event but a process.

This concept needs explanation. If you go to an event such as a dance or a football match, its after-effects are minimal (unless you are Cinderella!). Once the event is over, that's it. A divorce is totally different. You get your divorce on a certain date, which has some legal and financial implications, but afterwards there is still a long process of adjustment. This normally becomes less intense over the years, but, in a sense, the after-effects of divorce are lifelong. Hence, divorce is not an event but a process.

A word of encouragement

These points are grim and well worth taking very seriously indeed. However, Christians worship a God of light and love so don't despair. If you are going to be involved in a divorce, the remaining chapters are to assist and encourage you on the sad journey through. It is a false friend who doesn't point out the perils of the journey beforehand.

5 Professional Help

Once divorce proceedings begin they are very hard to stop. They develop their own momentum; it is downhill all the way. So, before you begin, think over all the difficulties long and hard. Ask yourself, 'Have I really done all I can? Have I really put the children first? All in all, won't I be worse off at the end of the day?' As a Christian, you will have the added responsibility of asking yourself, 'What does God think about all this?'

Remember that reconciliation is always possible, even at the very last moment. A few years ago, our whole church was immensely encouraged by a reconciliation. Briefly, a young couple, after a happy start, drifted apart. The wife went to live with someone else many miles away from London while her husband, living alone, became a Christian. He had not seen his wife for over two years. Once converted, he determined to do all he could to save his marriage even though lawyers were involved and a decree of divorce was only days away. He prayed, he fasted, he persisted. Finally, he sent her two tickets to hear Billy Graham. The boyfriend wasn't able to go and the wife, amazingly, asked her estranged husband instead. They went. She was converted and, within a short while, they were reconciled and have remained together. This bald account does not do them justice; their story is considerably more moving than the bestseller *Love Story*. I doubt whether Hollywood, however, would be so keen to make it into a film! Such reconciliations are rare but inspiring.

Attitude

If divorce is inevitable, your attitude during the process can still make a considerable difference. Compare the finesse of a surgical operation to the dismembering of cattle in a slaughterhouse. As a student, I spent a year in the Argentine and, in Patagonia, visited a slaughterhouse where the sheep were driven in from the plains at one end and, in a remarkably short time, their bits and pieces came out the other end. It was a ruthless, bloody, messy business whereas a surgical operation requires infinite skill and patience. Are you going to be a surgeon or a butcher? Are you going to employ a surgeon or a butcher? Even if your marriage is irretrievably on the rocks, it is still a vital relationship. It still has some life in it so, clearly, a surgeon is better than a butcher.

If you view your marriage as a house you are now faced with the problem of dismantling your house, of literally pulling it down. You can either do this carefully, with as little damage to you and your children as possible or you can knock it down with a ball and chain. Which is better? If you are pressing for a divorce, you can set the tone of the whole proceeding. Even if you do not want a divorce, your attitude and your reactions can usually still have considerable impact. The main difficulty is that you are called upon to be fair and reasonable when your life is in ruins and you are pressed on all sides.

Solicitors

If you have only been married a short time, have very few assets and no children, you may well not need a solicitor. Normally, a solicitor's help is required. You should choose your solicitor with great care. The family solicitor who dealt with Granny's will or that nice young man who conveyed your flat four years ago may well not be the answer: their expertise does not lie in divorce. Clearly, you require an experienced divorce solicitor but there is more to it than that. Personalities matter. You should not choose the most sympathetic solicitor nor the most aggressive. Why not? If your solicitor is too sympathetic then, when the crunch comes, he or she may well not be able to take a wholly professional, independent and objective view. On the other hand, if he or she is too aggressive then you may well find yourself plunged into expensive litigation when a more sensible and tolerant approach would have settled the matter, at less cost and less pain to all concerned.

Above all, you must respect your solicitor and your solicitor must respect you. Your self-respect is low at this time but you are the client and, as such, you are entitled to have your case done your way. On the other hand, in many ways, you are in a patient/doctor relationship so you need to rely on somebody who, if the occasion warrants it, is able to stand up to you. There is a wise old saying that 'a lawyer who acts for himself has a fool for a client'. Your solicitor must retain objectivity and your respect. Above all, find an experienced competent solicitor of integrity, both of you being on the same wavelength. If your solicitor suggests a counsellor first, follow that advice.

Watch their bills: a few solicitors and barristers charge exorbitant fees, thereby radically reducing the family assets. A case was recently reported in which approximately one-third of the family assets had been spent on litigation. Admittedly, the parties were rich but, all the same, surely it is better to spend the money within the family, particularly if you have children, rather than outside it. Of course, sometimes you have to go to court; but normally with experienced lawyers, it can be avoided. If you have very little money, Legal Aid may help you.

By far the best course is to ask around your friends and acquaintances who have been through a divorce themselves.

Counsellors

The word 'counsellor' sounds formidable. A counsellor can range from a good friend right up to a professionally qualified psychiatrist. Fortunately most of us will not require such qualified help. If we do, then follow the general approach suggested for solicitors and, except in the rarest of circumstances, once you have found your expert stick with that person. Here we are more concerned with the middle range of counsellor. Some of these may be mature members of the church who, quite informally, have become involved. Others may have had some training from such organisations as Relate or may have taken a course run by their local church or by a larger group of churches. Experience, maturity, common sense count but so does training; ideally, try and find a counsellor with both.

Whether you are a churchgoer or not, may I diffidently say this: there are many admirable non-Christians who can help and advise you. All the same, take great care. You are vulnerable and there are fakes and charlatans around.

Incidentally, sometimes I come across people who are constantly changing their solicitors. There may be good reasons but, generally speaking, there aren't. Likewise, people who constantly change their advisers are not doing themselves much good. For one thing, it may suggest that they are not able to take sound advice. For another, confusion may well occur. As with any marriage problem, you must have a consistent strategy.

A few obvious points: as with solicitors, you must respect your counsellor. From time to time, the advice may be hard to swallow. You are not a child and the pill cannot always be sugar coated, but if you respect your counsellor you are more likely to do what you are told. Usually, your counsellor should be your age or older. Not that we all get wiser with age – far from it! All the same, if you are forty, coping with three children and an unfaithful husband, you may well find the well-meaning advice of an unmarried twenty-three-year-old verging on the unrealistic.

Some years ago, before our church had fully developed its counselling ministry, accidents happened. My wife and I still recall wincing when a naïve, indeed ignorant, person was purporting to advise someone who was facing substantial problems. This 'advice' was only making matters worse. Normally, your counsellor should be of the same sex, otherwise there is a danger of emotional involvement which will damage you both. You may prefer to have counselling with a couple, sometimes married, sometimes not. Sadly, in some situations, you may not be able to have any counselling at all, hence the justification for this and other books. We have found that two minds are often better than one and what shocks my wife bores me, whereas she rightly sees significance in something which I have dismissed as trivial. Only a few weeks ago an acquaintance casually said six words to us which were more revealing than all that had been said over the preceding weeks. Later events have conclusively proved this to be right.

You can counsel anywhere at any time. You may be chatting in the launderette or outside school or doing the washing-up or walking along the beach. The formal headmaster's study approach may well be very off-putting although, undoubtedly, there are times when this is the only way to bring matters to a head. May I stress that, as counsellor, you should always ask yourself, 'Am I up to this?' When Corrie ten Boom was a little girl in Holland she once asked her father a question of a sexual nature. Pointing to a heavy suitcase, he asked her whether she could lift it. 'No,' she replied, 'it is too heavy.' To which her wise father replied, 'So is your question, my dear. The answer is too heavy for you to carry at your age.' Likewise, if we cannot cope, the sooner we transfer to someone who can the better. Better for us and better for them.

Friends

Most of us, fortunately, do not need counsellors at all. We merely need friends. When divorce strikes, you will find that not all your old friends remain loyal. Some desert you out of embarrassment, the sheer inability to cope with their own emotions let alone yours. Others desert you for baser reasons. You no longer are as rich and successful or as much fun as you were before and they move on to richer pickings which may include your separated husband or wife. Either way, forget these people. There is no point in being bitter and, as a wise old friend told me during my divorce, far better to be shot of people like that if they are going to let you down in your hour of need. Moreover, contrast their disloyalty with the surprising and encouraging love and loyalty shown you by lesser friends or by people you have never met before. Looking back, I find that although I was hurt by the behaviour of some fair-weather friends, I can truly say that their loss was ultimately minimal. Moreover, far finer friends have replaced them.

During the actual divorce, it is prudent to surround yourself with a small loyal circle of friends. Jesus, in all the strains and stresses of his short ministry, surrounded himself with a small circle of intimates and, within that circle, was particularly close to a few. We should do the same, consciously choosing friends for their loyalty, their love and – dare I say it – their laughter. Keep your gloomy friends for when you are feeling stronger. If you have few friends or have recently moved to a new area, at least try to find someone, always avoiding emotional entanglements.

Chad Varah founded the Samaritans in 1953. They assist those contemplating suicide often by just listening to them on the telephone. It is now a large international organisation, dealing with 2.5 billion calls each year in the United Kingdom. When asked about volunteers, he had this to say: 'I would not have anyone who was prudish or preachy because the prudish want to sit in judgment and reject, which could drive people to suicide; the preachy want to talk instead of listen, they will not accept the person as he or she is.' He went on to say that the qualities he looked for were based on how he imagined he would feel if he were burdened with guilt or extreme unhappiness when facing that person. 'I ask myself: Could I tell it to that face' (*Independent*, April 30th, 1992).

Choose, if you can, that type of person for your small circle and within this small circle, be yourself. Tell them your pains and your pleasures without demanding more of them than they are able to give.

True friends?

Having built up your small circle of friends, always beware of false friends and acquaintances. You may well not have known them before and, if in good health and happiness, would have avoided them. Many of us can confirm that, in these times of crisis, such people come out of the wood-work, noting your weakness, seeing what they can get out of it. Usually in a mess themselves, they may seek your time, your money, your body. You are in no position to cope with such people so please don't give them an inch. If in doubt, ask your true friends. At this difficult time, your powers of discernment are not at their best: all the more reason to trust your true friends' advice.

It is very tempting to tell the world, particularly if you have been wronged. This temptation is almost overwhelming. Resist this temptation. There are many reasons why you should. First, you may reconcile. Second, badly as your partner has behaved, that person is still the parent of your children. Third, in Hebrews 4:12 we read, 'For the word of God is living and active . . . piercing to the division of soul and spirit, of joints and marrow, and discerning the thoughts and intentions of the heart.' In other words, the word of God has a life of its own. Conversely, so have evil thoughts and words. They do harm. Fourth, your complaints, even if justified, demean you. The truth will out. You don't have to shout it from the hilltops.

6   First-Aid When the Crunch Comes

The Owl and the Pussy-cat went to sea,
  In a beautiful pea-green boat.
They took some honey, and plenty of money,
  Wrapped up in a five-pound note.
                                    Edward Lear

The fraught early days of divorce require rather more preparation than this. You will find that your emotions will be running so high, your mood-swings so out of control, that the more preparations you can make beforehand the better. What's more, how you behave in these early days may well colour the rest of the divorce and will certainly have a bearing on how quickly or not you recover.

To start with, as far as you can, don't be rash. I'm assuming that the decision is irreversible and that most people reading this particular chapter are on the receiving end of a divorce. By rash, I mean don't do anything irrevocable. For example, you may rightly be in considerable anguish at being forced out of your home. But to damage that home before you are compelled to leave will gain you nothing. To abuse your unfaithful wife in front of the children will gain you nothing. To strike your drunken husband in front of your children will gain you nothing. Difficult though circumstances are, try not to make matters worse. You are more likely to follow this advice if you have made some preparations beforehand and, even then, you will be surprised at your own behaviour and reactions.

The value of prayer

These preparations are both spiritual and practical. Both are essential. To say, 'I have faith that God will see me right' without trying to find alternative accommodation first is folly. Likewise, just to concentrate on practical details alone, without any spiritual framework, is ignoring God, who is always able and willing to help us. James 2:14 is worth reading on the point of both faith and works.

Your spiritual preparation lies in prayer. Probably against your will, your marriage is now hopelessly on the rocks, unless a miracle intervenes. You will find it very hard indeed to pray. You will feel that God has let you down and that you have let God down. All the same, try to pray, asking him to be with you in your hour of need.

You can pray generally and specifically. Generally, pray for courage, for calmness, for confidence and for the children. Specifically, each day pray for help over specific problems. God loves us – so ask his help over mundane, minor details as well as the big issues. Nothing is too small or too big for God. In addition, if you can pray outside your own situation, praying for others as well as for yourself, you will find that this will assist you greatly. Apart from your daily Bible reading, if you can steel yourself to read some inspirational Christian book or, possibly, a Christian biography, so much the better. I have not attached a list of suggested books in this area, not least because one's moods vary so much at this time, but take a good look at your church bookstall. Hudson Taylor spreading the word in China over a hundred years ago, Jackie Pullinger doing the same among the drug addicts in modern Hong Kong, Corrie ten Boom, vibrantly alive in a Nazi concentration camp. The list goes on. The more you can detach yourself from the present misery of your situation, the better.

Our nineteenth-century ancestors were very keen on Bible texts. Up until a few years ago you could buy them for a few pounds in junk shops or at jumble sales: 'God is love', 'God bless this house', 'Blessed are the meek', all hand-embroidered in dark wood frames or printed in heavy gothic lettering. In many ways, our ancestors were very wise to do this and I attach a list of forty biblical references which you may find of assistance. You can either have the whole list photocopied for a noticeboard, or perhaps more usefully choose one or two texts you find particularly helpful and attach them with a magnet to the fridge or stick them on the mirror in the bathroom. Never underestimate the power of the word. Let it become part and parcel of you, however grim you may be feeling.

I AM . . .

1   A child of God (Rom. 8:16)
2   Redeemed from trouble (Ps. 107:2)
3   Forgiven (Col. 1:13–14)
4   Saved by grace through faith (Eph. 2:8)
5   Justified (Rom. 5:1)
6   Sanctified (1 Cor. 1:30)
7   A new creation (2 Cor. 5:17)
8   A partaker of his divine nature (2 Pet. 1:4)
9   Redeemed from the curse of the law (Gal. 3:13)
10 Delivered from the powers of darkness (Col. 1:13)
11 Led by the Spirit of God (Rom. 8:14)
12 A son of God (Rom. 8:14)
13 Guarded by angels (Ps. 91:11)
14 Getting all my needs met by Jesus (Phil. 4:19)
15 Casting all my cares on God (1 Pet. 5:7)
16 Strong in the Lord and in the strength of his might (Eph. 6:10)
17 Doing all things in Christ who strengthens me (Phil. 4:13)
18 An heir of God and a joint heir with Jesus (Rom. 8:17)

19 Heir to the blessing of Abraham (Gal. 3:14)
20 Observing and doing the Lord's commandments (Deut. 28:13)
21 Blessed coming in and blessed going out (Deut. 28:6)
22 An heir of eternal life (1 John 5:11–12)
23 Blessed with all spiritual blessings (Eph. 1:3)
24 Healed by his wounds (1 Pet. 2:24)
25 Exercising my authority over the enemy (Luke 10:19)
26 Above only and not beneath (Deut. 28:13)
27 More than a conqueror (Rom. 8:37)
28 Establishing God's word here on earth (Matt. 16:19)
29 An overcomer by the blood of the Lamb and the word of my testimony (Rev. 12:11)
30 Daily overcoming the devil (1 John 4:4)
31 Looking to unseen things that are eternal (2 Cor. 4:18)
32 Walking by faith and not by sight (2 Cor. 5:7)
33 Destroying all obstacles to the knowledge of God (2 Cor. 10:5)
34 Bringing every thought into captivity (2 Cor. 10:5)
35 Being transformed by renewing my mind (Rom. 12:2)
36 God's fellow worker (1 Cor. 3:9)
37 The righteousness of God in Christ (2 Cor. 5:21)
38 An imitator of God (Eph. 5:1)
39 The light of the world (Matt. 5:14)
40 Blessing the Lord at all times and continually praising him (Ps. 34:1)

Practical considerations

By now, I assume you will have obtained some professional advice and will not take any important steps without it. Suffice it to say, questions such as, 'Where am I going to live?', 'What am I going to live on?' and 'What is to be done with the children?' should be worked out well in advance.

If you are fleeing the family home because life is so intolerable or if you are being pushed out of your home, you must have alternative accommodation available. What is more, such accommodation must be reasonable for your needs and you really cannot expect either your friends or family to have you indefinitely. It is often a great assistance to have accommodation on standby and available for a few months. During those few months, more permanent plans can be made.

As for income, very often your ability to earn and/or your partner's ability or willingness to pay go into a sharp decline. The most surprising people have found themselves having to live on state benefits while these problems are resolved. It may be very difficult but if your marriage is likely to end in separation and divorce, it is as well to try and build up some ability to earn before the actual break comes. Very often, if you are a deserted woman with dependent children your skills are rusty and your availability very limited, but any efforts you can make to help yourself are worth doing, both for practical reasons and for your own morale.

As for the children, as stressed again and again, they are the priority. Whatever your own pain in these early days, they must be considered. It is very damaging to take them, without warning, away from the only home, area and school they know. In rare emergencies, this may be necessary. If you are putting them first, you may well have to propose certain plans until contingency arrangements are in hand. The more links you can keep unbroken the better. In other words, if you have to move away from home, it is better to stay in the same area, at least for a while, so that the children will still be able to see their friends, go to the same school and (whatever your feelings) probably see the other parent. Children dislike change, as Julia Tugendhat's invaluable book, *What Teenagers Can Tell Us About Divorce And Stepfamilies*, makes very clear.

Helpers

The Holy Spirit is available twenty-four hours a day. At crisis time, as helpers, we should be the same, letting our friends know that, for a while at least, whatever the time of day and night, they have only to call and we will come. In fact, such offers are rarely taken up, thank goodness, but the very offer is of immense comfort to the person concerned. So, looking them straight in the eyes, tell them, 'Here we are – here's our phone number – just call or phone whenever you feel the need.'

My mother, now eighty-seven, said recently how reassuring it was to know that, two doors away, were a couple who would be round in a moment should she ever be in trouble. With our divorcing friends, we must give them the same reassurance, always remembering that once the first crisis is past their demands are likely to lessen. In addition to this general reassurance, in these early stages practical help, often menial practical help, is more valuable than overt spiritual help. We will of course be praying for them, for the other partner and for their marriage and children (and we can quietly tell them so) but it may well be that offering to do the school run both ways or to bring supper round tonight or take the car to the garage is what they need at this time. Once the crisis is over, we can talk of the Lord.

As we read in James 2:15, 'If a brother or sister is ill-clad and in lack of daily food, and one of you says to them, "Go in peace, be warmed and filled," without giving them the things needed for the body, what does it profit?'

7 How Can I Help Myself?

Chapter 4 concentrated on the cost of divorce, not just the financial cost, though this may be considerable, but the emotional cost – all the pain, guilt, anger, loneliness, which divorce entails. This affects not only yourself but your family and friends and, above all, the main victims, the children. Faced with this grim catalogue, enough to depress the most stout-hearted, you may well ask, 'How can I help myself?' A very fair question. Mercifully, there is much you can do.

Love yourself

Learn to love yourself. You may never have loved yourself before. Many people don't. Or you may have to rebuild your self-esteem. Either way it is a slow process but infinitely worth undertaking. Start now. Learn to love yourself. In Matthew 22, when Jesus was asked what was the greatest commandment, he replied: 'You shall love the Lord your God with all your heart, and with all your soul, and with all your mind. This is the first and great commandment. And a second is like it, You shall love your neighbour as yourself. On these two commandments depend all the law and the prophets' (vv. 37–40).

So, love yourself. We are not endorsing pride or conceit, which almost always end in tears. Think of silly, selfish Toad in *The Wind In The Willows* and how often he ended up in trouble! We are talking here of fostering a feeling of self-value, self-esteem, self-worth. Your spouse may have reduced you to pulp but your family, your friends, your colleagues and, supremely, God, value you. You are made in God's image. You are his child. He loves you. You are unique; you have a unique contribution to make.

Therefore, step by step, inch by inch, you must rebuild your confidence. Of course outsiders and time can help this process but ultimately it is up to you. In human terms, as Rudyard Kipling says, 'The race is run by one and one.' So, brick by brick, rebuild yourself rather differently, perhaps even better than you were before. After all, you will be both older and wiser. Taking the building analogy a little further, please remember the doors and windows as well. In other words let light into your building. There is no point in building a closed self-righteous bitter cell, imprisoning yourself within it.

Blame

At this difficult time, you may be helped and encouraged by a passage from James Dobson which I have successfully quoted at various divorce recovery seminars. It goes as follows:

The blame for marital disintegration is seldom the fault of the husband or wife alone. It takes two to tangle, as they say, and there is always some measure of shared blame for a divorce. However, when one marriage partner makes up his mind to behave irresponsibly, to become involved extramaritally, or to run from his family commitments and obligations, he usually seeks to justify his behaviour by magnifying the failures of his spouse. 'You didn't meet my needs, so I had to satisfy them somewhere else' is the familiar accusation. By increasing the guilt of his partner in this way, he reduces his own culpability. For a husband or wife with low self-esteem, these charges and recriminations are accepted as fact when hurled his way. 'Yes it was my fault. I drove you to it.' Thus the victim assumes the full responsibility for his partner's irresponsibility, and self-worth shatters (*Doctor Dobson Answers Your Questions*, Kingsway Publications, 1983).

Doctor Dobson goes on to encourage you to examine the facts carefully and objectively. Try to answer these questions now, although you may well find that you can answer them fairly only after a decent lapse of time.

1   Despite my human frailties, did I value my marriage and try to preserve it?
2   Did my partner decide to destroy it and then seek justification?
3   Was I given a fair chance to resolve the areas of greatest irritation?
4   Could I have held my partner even if I had made all the changes wanted?

Doctor Dobson wisely adds,

You should know that social rejection breeds feelings of inferiority and self-pity in enormous proportions. And rejection by the one you love, particularly, is the most powerful destroyer of self-esteem in the entire realm of human experience. You might begin to see yourself as a victim in this process, rather than a worthless failure at the game of love.

On a personal note, if I had had these four questions pinned to my shaving-mirror when I was in distress and had answered them truthfully, I would have recovered my balance and my happiness far sooner. The victims nearly always take upon themselves the guilt of the guilty – so put it back where it belongs.

A grief situation

Appreciate that you are grieving. At the time, I did not consciously realise this. If I had, I am sure that I would have recovered more quickly. Consider somebody recently widowed after years of happy marriage and that it takes months, even years, to 'recover' from the death. You are in the same position but with two additional handicaps. To start with, your memories of your spouse are not sanctified by death, they are tainted by divorce. Second, society will rally round the widowed, at least for a while. You will receive little or no such support.

Furthermore, our Western society does not handle grief wisely although this is improving. Particularly if we are men we are taught to hide our grief and to put on a bold face, 'stiff upper lip and all that'. To a very limited extent this may have its uses. All the same, we must express our grief and pain. We must be prepared to work through it. We must weep and be angry, even rant and rave – for a while – and then *stop*. If we don't work through our own grief, we are only stirring up trouble for ourselves later. Illness, depression, suicide can result from suppressed grief and anger.

A friend ten years after the death of a child suddenly exploded in grief for that child. At the time of the death she had been very brave but, internally, had not worked it out. Just as poignantly, I recall another person who lost a child well over twenty years before and was still, even to the casual observer, not recovered.

Again, thinking of the widowed, recall how strangely they can behave with their ups and downs, their good days and their bad. Our situation is analogous without the social support which the widowed rightly get. So, while in this grief situation, be kind to yourself. During mine, I said, did, and thought things which were totally out of character, with violent swings of mood, elation being followed by despair all in the space of a few minutes. It was as if I had lost a protective outer skin, making me hypersensitive, laughter one moment, tears the next. This passed. While you are going through this natural and healthy process which leads to healing, try to be objective, saying to yourself, 'This will pass.' After all, after an operation and illness we look after ourselves, we convalesce. Healing takes time. Above all, be PATIENT.

Five years

On the length of time it can take, I have no wish to depress. Christians should encourage. However, five years is a useful yardstick, meaning five years from the start of the irrevocable flaw in your marriage to the time, well after your divorce, that you can truly say, 'It is over. I am okay.' So, if you are reading this book and divorce is under way, you could already be halfway through the five-year period and it is by no means all gloom and doom. Remember, too, the speed of your recovery to health and happiness is partly up to you. Some recover in three years; others don't in a lifetime. You can choose. Avoid too quick a recovery. Likewise avoid too slow a recovery.

Self-pity

Avoid self-pity like the plague. Appreciate that others have problems; learn and listen to their problems. I certainly didn't follow this advice. As Dobson points out, 'bitterness and resentment are emotional cancers which rot us from within.' Self-pity is a malignant tumour.

Maya Angelou, the bestselling American author, has had an eventful life. She has been a prostitute, a madam, the first black conductor on the San Francisco street cars, a mother at sixteen, Creole cook, singer, dancer, star of *Porgy and Bess*, civil rights activist with Martin Luther King and is now a poet, university teacher and the bestselling black US female writer. When she was eight, she was raped by her mother's boyfriend. The man was lynched and beaten to death. For the next five years she didn't or couldn't speak and was repeatedly beaten by her family for 'refusing' to talk. She has this to say about bitterness. 'Bitterness doesn't do a damn thing. It is like a cancer which eats into his host. But anger is like fire' (*Independent*, March 23rd, 1992).

One invaluable cure is to look up to God. When you think of his greatness and goodness, when you think of Jesus and his sacrifice on the Cross, your own pressing problems fall into a better perspective. They do not go away but in a supernatural way, they get into proportion. Try it and see. Think of the happy tale of the old priest who said, 'I like swimming in the sea. When I lie on my back and look up to heaven I float but as soon as I look at my tummy button, I begin to sink!' Again, think of that splendid earthy man, Peter the fisherman, in Matthew 14:28–31, who walked on the water to Jesus when he trusted him. When he didn't, he began to sink. As Jesus said, 'O man of little faith, why did you doubt?'

Another simultaneous cure is to think of others and, believe me, there are always people worse off than you. They desperately need and deserve your help. Thanks be to God, by helping them, you will help yourself. There is no doubt about this. Time and time again I have seen this come true. Reach out to help others and, almost without your noticing, your own problems become less daunting.

Where to help? The opportunities are endless. Often your own family, neighbours and friends and your church provide a start. A telephone call, a letter, a short visit can produce pleasure out of all proportion to your effort. Looking more widely, what about local charities if you are very busy, or national charities if you have more time? I am not suggesting a heavy involvement. It is probably not a good idea at this stage but some effort to help others will help you tenfold. Incidentally, choose an enjoyable form of help. If you dislike cooking, don't. If you love sewing, do. Activities which bring you into contact with people are preferable to addressing a thousand envelopes in a lonely bedsitter.

Dame Barbara Cartland, aged ninety, has two main claims to fame. She is the step-grandmother of the Princess of Wales and she is the world's most famous romantic novelist, having written over 550 books. I must be one of the few men who have read one, namely *A Virgin in Mayfair* – an unforgettable experience. She is a very active and remarkable old lady and her advice to lonely people? 'Go to the town hall, ask for a list of charities and join everything. They will all be delighted to have you. When you have made a few friends you can drop the rest' (*BUPA Magazine*, Winter 1992). In many ways, she has got it right.

Hobbies

Consider taking up some hobby or interest which is neither demanding nor expensive to help break the emotional logjam. This is very therapeutic and, under God, you must be your own physician. Avoid heavy or difficult commitments. Better an evening class in Chinese cooking than starting a five-year course in Mandarin. Better a cycling weekend in France with your brother than joining the Foreign Legion. In other words, get yourself involved in enjoyable lightweight interests which will bring you out of yourself. These hobbies need not be expensive. The library or town hall will undoubtedly help. With some diffidence, I offer a list of possibilities. I have no doubt at all that you can draw up a better list. You could consider aerobics, cooking, cycling, dancing, embroidery, gardening, jogging, knitting, languages, music, museums, painting, reading, swimming, singing or walking.

Of course, parents with little money and young children will find it very difficult to take up any outside interest; survival is difficult enough. All the same remember what many people have achieved against the odds. Reading recent obituaries, often of people involved in the Second World War, I am humbled by what people have done against almost overwhelming odds.

Laughter

Recently the newspapers mentioned a new remedy for countering stress and despair being pioneered in inner city Birmingham. The treatment costs nothing, has no harmful side-effects, its applications are virtually limitless. It is called 'laughing'. Now you will say, 'How can he write such nonsense – here am I, with two kids, no husband, no money and no hope and he tells me to laugh – bah!' I can understand this point of view. I would have shared it for a while during my difficulties. However, even if at the moment you cannot solve your problems you can alter your attitude to them. Even in a divorce, laughter is possible and, quite deliberately, quite consciously, you must try and make room for it.

Various suggestions come to mind. One is to surround yourself with wholesome, cheerful, happy people as far as you possibly can. They should not be superficial. The danger is that at a time of crisis, grim vultures circle round and round the dying marriage. You are indeed very vulnerable. Some of these people ('I know what it's like . . . I've been through it myself . . . they're all the same . . . of course I've always said . . . ') may mean well. Some don't mean well at all, getting some sick pleasure out of your distress and more practically seeing what pickings are to be had. We all have friends, acquaintances, even family like this. Avoid these people as far as you can. Firmly and politely show them the door. If you are going to retain any buoyancy at all you can't afford to let them drag you down.

Not only choose happy friends but also happy events as far as you can. I speak as one who read Thomas Hardy on his honeymoon – not wise! Your divorce apart, it is possible to avoid some depressing situations and certainly you can shield your children from them. Better a picnic in the country or in the park than a gloomy film in a dirty cinema. Likewise, with books or films or videos, choose ones which inspire and encourage and entertain, which help to lighten your load.

This leads me to fun. I well recall, in the depths of my divorce, visiting the Portobello Road market in London. The sun shone, the stalls glistened, the crowd swarmed and there was an eccentric old woman pretending to be Vera Lynn holding an old radio in front of her face – and for ten minutes or so, I was completely happy. Quite taken out of myself, just having fun. Poets can do better justice to this mood than I. But the point is that we can quite deliberately place ourselves and our children in situations where fun, laughter, humour are more likely to occur. Do it.

A word of warning. Of course, grief has to be worked through and many practical problems have to be worked out and faced. It is very unwise to stifle either grief or reality. Moreover, humour should not be used artificially like anaesthetic or drink or drugs. It should rather be a pick-up, a boost on a difficult journey. We have all met people who, tragically, never face up to life. I recently saw, in one week, two very famous comedians on the London Underground. Even allowing for the fact that they were off duty, they had two of the most miserable, even tortured, faces I have ever seen.

Sufficient unto the day

In Matthew 6:34 Jesus said, 'Therefore do not be anxious about tomorrow, for tomorrow will be anxious for itself. Let the day's own trouble be sufficient for the day.' Even when life is going well most of us find this hard to do – and it is much harder when life is not going well. 'How can I live for today and forget tomorrow when the bailiffs may repossess next week or he'll be violent tonight or she'll be out with that man again?' How indeed? It is very difficult but this is what the Bible says. Moreover, as explained later, God will provide you with considerable help.

A few months ago, as an observer, I attended a meeting

of Alcoholics Anonymous. The evening was very moving, with men and women of differing ages and backgrounds all showing what drink had done to them and how much better they were without it. Their essential message was to take each day at a time. They never said they were cured of alcoholism – apart from a miracle, there is no cure – they merely said that day, that twenty-four hours, they had not drunk and they would not drink. Try and adopt their courageous attitude.

The AA prayer is worth memorising: 'God grant me the serenity to accept the things I cannot change, the courage to change the things I can and the wisdom to know the difference.'

Deep emotional relationships

Don't yet! This is explored later. At the moment, I can only urge you to accept that you are in no fit state to take on any deep relationship. The world, the flesh and the devil will combine to suggest that you have only to find someone else and sleep with them for most, if not all, of your problems to disappear. This is just not so. In the short run, the very short run, you may indeed find that your pain is temporarily anaesthetised. Beware. If you continue with the second relationship, there is a very high chance indeed that not only will you make it all the harder honourably to end your first relationship but the jagged edges from your first relationship will seriously harm your second.

Time and time again, we come across people who are in difficulties with their second relationship which are partly, if not overwhelmingly, caused by the unresolved difficulties of their first.

Prayer

In 1 Thessalonians 5:17 we are told to pray constantly. We know that God answers prayers. A few years ago, when I was sitting on the London Underground reading a book of that very title, *God Answers Prayers*, an old lady tapped me on the knee and said, 'He does, my dear, but sometimes the answer is no!' Quite right, but, as Christians, we believe that everything works together for good for those that love God and are called according to his purposes. God knows best. As John Wesley frequently said, 'God has bound himself to do nothing save in answer to prayer.' So pray. Lift up to God your pain and problem. Be honest with him and tell him how much you are hurting and he will hear and he will help. Jesus knows all about suffering. He suffered on the Cross so that if we believe in him we might be free from the consequences of our own sin.

If you are not so committed a Christian, I would still recommend prayer. God is there, hearing your prayers even if you don't yet accept him, and there can be no harm, only good, in asking his help.

Forgiveness

The central message of this book is forgiveness. If you throw it away and forget all it says there is no harm done if you remember forgiveness. The clue to recovery from divorce is no more no less than forgiveness. Work through your anger and then start to forgive.

There are three essential points to make: first, we ourselves have been forgiven so much. As Psalm 103:12 reminds us, 'as far as the east is from the west, so far does he remove our transgressions from us'. Jesus died on the Cross to pay the price of our sins such that if we believe in him we shall have eternal life. If we repent of our sins, however bad they are, we are forgiven. If we have been forgiven, we must ourselves forgive. Remember the parable of the unjust steward, Matthew 18:23–35. His master forgave him an enormous debt yet he refused to forgive a minor debt and as such was cast into prison. Yes, we have something to forgive but, compared with what God has forgiven us, it is minor and we must forgive. This is not an optional extra for a Christian. It is a divine command. Again, Matthew 18:21–2, ' "Lord, how often shall my brother sin against me, and I forgive him? As many as seven times?" Jesus said to him, "I do not say to you seven times, but seventy times seven." ' Please read that passage.

Second, and this is obvious because God's commands are for our own well-being, we must forgive for our own health and happiness. In other words, bitterness harms us. It eats away at our entrails. It corrodes us and it stops us from moving on with life in a happy and healthy way. Surely all of us know people whose bitterness has ruined their own lives and marred the lives of all with whom they come in contact, including their children. Someone once graphically said, 'You can smell the bitterness.' Therefore, if you are not a Christian and cannot accept my first point then, for your own sake, accept this second.

Third, forgiveness is a decision, an act of will, not a feeling. On God's orders and with his help, you decide to forgive even if emotionally (most understandably) you can't. This is very important to understand. In the end, your emotions will follow your intellect. You will forgive with your head as well as your heart but you will have to start with your head. As Christians, we will find that the Holy Spirit will help the process immensely so we should pray to be able to forgive and, likewise, others should pray for us. Difficult but – praise the Lord – possible and infinitely worth doing. The more you forgive, the more your bitterness decreases. You feel lighter and freer – it unblocks the drains.

It helps to remember that even if you are the innocent party you are not without some blame yourself, however slight the proportion may be at least in your mind. You have sinned and you must repent of your sins. You can do nothing about your partner's sins. That is between your partner and God. Leave it to God. In the meantime, with prayer, repent and put your own house in order. Remember St Paul in Romans 3:22–3, 'there is no distinction;

since all have sinned and fall short of the glory of God.'

A prayer

For your own health and happiness why not try praying along these lines? – 'I'm sorry for what I've done; please forgive me for my part in the breakdown.' Then, trying hard to be honest both to yourself and to God, why not continue, 'At the moment, as you know I can't forgive, it hurts so much. Please, God, help me to forgive. I can't do it in my own strength. It's just too hard.' Then, trying to remember the good points of your partner and of your marriage, 'Please, God, help me to remember the good points about A and the good times we had in our marriage. Thank you for all the love we used to have and all the fun we had together. Thank you for laughter, thank you for his courage . . . thank you for the way he worked so hard . . . thank you for her skill . . . thank you for her undoubted love for the children.'

Now, attempt to forgive your partner in a small way. *Here a little, there a little.* For the moment, you are not yet able to forgive the adultery so how about forgiving the occasional bad temper, the persistent lateness, the refusal to answer important letters and the insistence of leaving the television on, even when friends or family were around. These are minor points but you have to start somewhere.

Finally, and this may take many weeks, even months, start forgiving the major wrongs done to you. Fortified by prayer, just forgive, thereby releasing not only your partner but also yourself. Like a bird freed from a net, you will be able to fly free again.

Postscript

A few weeks ago, in a divorce recovery seminar, about twenty of us were praying about forgiveness – and a picture came into my mind: I saw an iceberg (unforgiveness) floating in an icy sea. I remembered that an iceberg had sunk the *Titanic* in 1912 – then the sun (God's love) began to shine, and imperceptibly, the iceberg melted, the sea became warmer, until the iceberg had entirely melted away.

8 How Can Outsiders Help?

Therefore, take the whole armour of God, that you may be able to withstand in the evil day, and having done all, to stand. Stand therefore, having girded your loins with truth, and having put on the breastplate of righteousness, and having shod your feet with the equipment of the gospel of peace; besides all these, taking the shield of faith, with which you can quench all the flaming darts of the evil one. And take the helmet of salvation, and the sword of the Spirit, which is the word of God. Pray at all times in the Spirit, with all prayer and supplication (Eph. 6:13–18).

Put on prayer

Before going into battle it is wise to be properly armed. If we are going to help people through a divorce we must be prepared. Otherwise, either our help will be limited or, more seriously, we ourselves will be bruised and even damaged by the encounter. Unquestionably we will be attacked ourselves so, whether you are going to help as an individual, a couple or a group, always pray. The more prayer the better.

Before leading a seminar, giving a Christian talk or helping on a small mission around the country, I often find that I am at my worst, being assailed by bad temper, bad thoughts or just plain tiredness and indifference. Now that I appreciate that these are indeed 'the wiles of the devil' I am more able to cope, putting on the armour of God.

You are going into battle. In Lord Macaulay's stirring poem, you may recall that brave Horatius stood on the bridge, valiantly keeping the enemy at bay. In a sense that is what you are going to do, protecting the wounded victim from further attacks. If you find Horatius rather old hat, then how about Charlton Heston in *Ben Hur* or Ian Fleming's James Bond?

Fortified by prayer, do help all you can. There is no doubt that your help is needed even if it is not appreciated or even acknowledged. The victim is in great pain and wounded animals do tend to bite the hand that feeds them (with the notable exception of Dr Doolittle). They have lost their best friend, their other half, and need your help considerably. It may be needed, with lessening intensity, for a good many years. If you are going to help, you should see the problem through to the end, not the bitter end but the happy end.

An American friend once gently chided us, 'Beware of spreading yourself too thinly.' Better to help a few well than many inadequately. This is a problem because life does not bring people to you in neat intervals. They always seem to turn up at the wrong moment. All I can suggest is that while you should never turn down an immediate cry for help, it is as well to have a discreet filter system on hand, such that you can refer the person to somebody else. It is always very rewarding when you are able to refer people for help to those who only a short while ago were themselves in trouble. They often make fine helpers.

So the need for help is obvious, but how best to do this?

Love in action – the art of listening

Start by remembering that Christians should love one another. The Christian gospel is one of love: 1 John 3:11, 'we should love one another'. We are helping out of love, not judgmentally or inquisitively or patronisingly but out of love. Our brother, our sister, is hurt and we wish to help.

Initially this usually involves listening and listening and listening. Often, to endless repetition, inaccuracies and distortions, sometimes even to obscenities. But you must just listen at this stage. For some people you may find that they require intense listening in a formal atmosphere, i.e. the study door closed, you behind your desk, the person in front of your desk. With others, this format would not work and they may well only unburden themselves if you go for a walk with the dog or do the washing-up together. It is essential to be as approachable as possible. You may even have to initiate the conversation on the lines of 'You are looking awfully tired' or 'I am sorry that David/Diana can't come to lunch tomorrow.'

Simultaneously, listen to God. When listening to God either by praying or by being open to him, you can still be walking, even talking. Don't put people off by obvious prayer unless they specifically ask for it.

Some of us are better listeners than others. As a lawyer I dislike repetitions, distortions and inaccuracies. My whole training is precision. I know that 'they met in Singapore', why tell me again and again? I know that 'he was made bankrupt in 1982' – why tell me again and again?

Three points may help. First, remember that by merely listening, you are fulfilling a therapeutic purpose. They are being helped towards healing by getting it off their chests, a little like lancing a boil. Second, you can learn a good deal about the situation by noting what they do stress and what they don't. In other words, if Singapore and bankruptcy are important to her then they are important to you. Try and pick up the emotional picture. You can always get the factual picture later, either from the victim when calmer or from elsewhere. Third, if you are not a good listener, you can enable others to listen. Thus, on occasions, I'll relieve my wife Caroline by taking the children out for a walk or giving them a bath so that she can listen in peace. She is much better at this. Afterwards, if the other person agrees, we can then discuss it together.

Confidentiality

This leads to confidentiality. Confidentiality is vital. The person must feel that secrets will be kept secret. Even if some of them are little secrets, if told in confidence, they must remain in confidence. This is easier said than done particularly with 'minor' confidences. You probably wouldn't tell the world that they had been abused as a child but you might well let slip that they ate six Mars bars a day. Both are breaches of trust. Indeed, in some situations, they might be as hurt by the one disclosure as the other. So take confidentiality seriously. Beware of praying out loud in groups, 'Please Lord, help Michael over his drinking' – but no one knew about his drinking until you prayed out loud!

Sometimes, of course, you want to discuss this matter with other people. If so, always ask the person if this is in order, even whether you can tell your husband or your wife or minister. Usually, if they trust you and know why you want a second opinion, they will agree but you must ask first.

An urgent plea to the older generation

Some of us blessed with growing families and responsible jobs don't have so much time to listen. Once we know the facts we can help swiftly and practically but our time and energies are limited. Those retired can be involved here. They have the time and they have the wisdom. In our flourishing church, Holy Trinity, Brompton, in London, with hundreds in the morning and hundreds in the evening, how we long for more grandparents – wise grandparents that is. Both my wife and I are in constant touch with our own parents. Their experience and advice is invaluable even if, at times, we don't always follow it!

There is a real ministry waiting to be taken up by the healthy, retired people in your church.

Acceptance

If you listen you must accept people as they are. By this, I don't mean that you should condone or encourage the sin but you should always love the sinner. You are a sinner, so am I. So when listening to whatever filth comes out, always try to get them to realise that you love them and, much more importantly, that God loves them. The very confession of sin by them to you brings it into the open and into the light, so in one sense its evil effect has diminished even if there is still work to be done. So don't interrupt. Give them the space and the time.

This acceptance can be very difficult. Whereas some sins such as mild violence, drinking, even adultery, may well be within our range of experience (either personal or general) others are not. Except in a professional capacity, I have never met anyone who has committed incest or murder. If told, what would I do? I frankly don't know.

This leads to a further important point. If the problem is too big for you to handle (and some problems are) then, firmly but lovingly you must decline to handle it. If you don't decline, you will not help the victim and you could well hurt yourself. In these rare instances, I would suggest saying the following, 'John/Jane, thank you for telling me. I still love/like you but I can't handle this alone. Let's go and see X and I will stay with you for as long as you need me. I won't let you and the family down. I am sure X can help.' What is more, you should not only follow up this promise but, in normal social ways, you should keep up with them lest they think they have been dropped because of their confession. You haven't dropped them as sinners but you have dropped their sin – it is too heavy for you to carry. Every church should have a discreet list of people well versed in major problems.

Only a few weeks ago, in a different context, I encountered this problem head on. A friend arrived out of the blue who was obviously mentally ill. I had just come home from work and my wife and children were milling around waiting for tea. He had recently been released from a mental hospital and, clearly to my lay eyes, the sooner he got back there the better. What could I do? Fighting back a mounting feeling of helplessness, I resolved that, come what may, I would stand by him until I got him back into the safety of hospital. It took over five hours to do so – red tape galore – but it worked and, by 10 p.m., I was home and he was safe. I didn't attempt to help beyond that because I just didn't know what to do. Let the professionals handle it as, indeed, in this case they did to a happy conclusion.

Encouragement

Throughout our helping, we should always try to encourage. As 1 Thessalonians 5:11 reminds us, 'encourage one another and build one another up'. Our friends' self-esteem has been shattered, their lives are in ruins. We should always try to encourage them, helping them to rebuild their lives and the lives of their children. Such encouragement should never be facile. It is neither honest nor kind to say that 'he'll give up drinking' or 'she'll come back' when they won't. It has been well said that a person who maintains a resolve to abandon a marriage will not be dragged by God, kicking and screaming, back into the relationship. All the same you can stand by them in their hour of need, gently, quietly suggesting that there is light and life at the end of the tunnel. You can help them rebuild their own dignity.

Normally, we are only called upon to minister to the 'victim', the so-called 'innocent party'. In my experience the 'guilty' party tends to avoid, like the plague, any friend or relation who might try to dissuade them from breaking up the marriage. They will run the proverbial mile rather than face anyone who may tell them to behave honourably. All the same, they have their problems even if they richly deserve some of them and we should love and encourage them without in any way condoning or encouraging their bad behaviour. This distinction is sometimes fine but essentially we must continue to love them. Although they may not know it now their behaviour may well end in disaster, even if years later. If you have negative feelings towards them then turn to Jesus, praying that he will give you the right touch at the right time. Remember how firmly yet gently he treated people who had failed.

In John 8:3–11, consider how Jesus dealt with the woman caught in adultery. He didn't condemn her but, be it noted, he added, 'Do not sin again.' Likewise his treatment of the woman at the well in John 4:7–30, where he loved her but not her behaviour.

It is so easy to be judgmental. Indeed, I only have to read the newspaper to find condemnation rising in my gorge. 'How can he do that?' 'How can she do this?' – and the breakfast table quivers!

Some years ago, a friend whom I liked and admired behaved very badly to his wife. For six months, I was so angry that I felt quite unable to speak to him at all except when I had to. However, I eventually realised that this attitude was 'holier than thou' and not helping at all. I began to see him again. He was not reconciled to his wife and our friendship is not as it was before, yet it still has some value and I dare say I am the only active Christian he and his new wife know.

The point is we must not be judgmental. As Romans 3:23 reminds us, 'all have sinned and fall short of the glory of God'. '. . . what about that beam in your eye?' (Matt. 7:3). We all have a tendency to disapprove of people whose failings have some relationship to our own failings. Before we criticise the sinner we should take a long hard look at ourselves. We are entitled to hate the sin and to judge the sin but not the sinner. At times this distinction, particularly outside Christian circles, is very hard to appreciate.

Furthermore, in some cases the more you know the parties concerned the harder it becomes to discover the truth, or at least, the rights and wrongs. 'Yes, he has been violent, that is wrong. Yet, what about her behaviour?' 'Yes, she has committed adultery, that is wrong. Yet what about his behaviour?'

Seeing both sides

Often, in helping we see only one of the couple. I well recall drafting a divorce petition in my chambers and being unusually appalled at the conduct of the husband towards his wife. It was appalling yet some months later, meeting the wife in court, I could understand what drove him to it. I was almost amazed at his moderation. Alternatively, later events may well justify reinterpreting earlier events. Thus, if you find that not only the first but the second and the third partner leave on the grounds of unreasonable behaviour, you may be driven to the conclusion that, despite outward charm, the person concerned is a little difficult to live with.

Finally, some practical considerations to consider. As the Bible and plain common sense tell us, there is no point trying to help people's spirits if they themselves are starving physically. When you have caught your finger in the door or have a raging toothache, can you concentrate on Scripture or is your whole being suffused with pain, obliterating everything else? Those in the middle of a divorce are in pain and, very often, their practical needs warrant immediate attention. Once these have been solved or at least alleviated, then you can help them emotionally or spiritually, but first things first. When I was going through a very rough time before I became a Christian, it was the cup of soup in the kitchen, the sympathetic ear, that brought me to Christ rather than overt preaching.

Let me share a few suggestions.

Money

Let's be blunt and talk money. One of the tragedies of divorce is that the cake cannot be cut into two cakes of similar size. Even the rich find out that their funds are not unlimited. The poor are hit all the harder and, so often, the weak go to the wall. We may well have to help financially and the main problem here is not so much appreciating this as finding ways to make our assistance palatable. People don't like charity. For the moment, I can only suggest that even small sums of money, whether anonymous or not, can work wonders, just like yeast. We are only trustees of our money. Let us use it as generously as we can. I am not advocating white lies because we should always strive to tell the truth, but if we can sugar the pill of our charity so much the better. Some minor examples spring quickly to mind – an aunt who sent a hundred pounds to her five nephews and nieces because an insurance policy had suddenly matured – a friend who arrived with seven bottles of wine, saying they were left over from a party – a friend arriving with an enormous casserole saying, 'Well, since I was making one, it seemed silly not to make another for you at the same time.'

Include them socially. Divorce is cruel in the way that it disrupts most social relationships and often those in the middle of a divorce suffer particularly badly. Their friends or acquaintances do not know where they stand or what to do with a result that they are dropped altogether. So, try to include them in parties and picnics and the like even if they are a little depressing and even if they usually refuse. Ask them all the same. The invitation matters. The old and widowed are likewise often ignored. Only the other day, my old mother put it very well: 'I like to be asked. I wouldn't have gone but I like to be asked.' Women suffer far more badly in this area than men.

Don't matchmake! It is neither kind nor sensible to put

additional pressure on people at this stage. Moreover, it usually doesn't work; your idea of Don Juan is not hers. The 'couple syndrome' has a good deal to answer for. Before you married, you often attended parties where the sexes were not evenly balanced. Once you are married, there is an increasing pressure to be neat and tidy socially, one husband, one wife, one husband, one wife, one husband, one wife, neatly round the supper table, with, perhaps, one unmarried pair for whom you have hopes. As Christians, we should surely do better than this. Just as human families are uneven in age and sex so should be the wider Christian family. Invite single people to your home, whether unmarried, widowed or divorced and don't worry if the numbers aren't right. This is particularly supportive to those going through a divorce because many people, both male and female, submerge their individual personalities in marriage, increasingly lacking independent identity. They are less well equipped to cope on their own than the single people who have had to paddle their own canoe for many years.

Then try to get them involved outside themselves by making gentle challenges. Often they are so wrapped up with their own problems (which may well be very difficult) that they just can't lift their heads up at all to look beyond the grim present to the possible future. You can help by making small challenges. 'Could you possibly give us an hour at the school fete' . . . 'Could you possibly umpire the children's tennis tournament' . . . these suggestions are not demanding. They are mild challenges and are intended to help the person build up damaged self-esteem. You should try to strike a balance between imposing on them and treating them as invalids. Consider those who care for the old, the invalid or the handicapped. If they do their job well, they never undermine their charges' dignity, always helping them to do their best, at the same time being there should they fail or fall.

Time

Also don't forget time. With your own husband's or wife's consent, you may have to spend some time helping them. Who is going to mow the lawn? Who is going to collect Granny from the station now that the car has got to be sold? Who is going to help Jane in puberty now that Mother is in Australia and Father has always been inordinately shy? The opportunities are endless. With just a little thought and a little time, five minutes here or five minutes there, great assistance can be given. Using your imagination, put yourself in their shoes. How are they going to cope? Specific help is often far more valuable than mere general benevolence.

In life's rough passages, I am more than ever convinced that small acts of kindness have a value out of all proportion to what is actually done or said. It is not too melodramatic to point out that potential suicides have changed their minds because of some small act of concern, sometimes from a complete stranger.

To summarise: armed with the whole armour of God, fortified by prayer, guided by the Holy Spirit, we should love those in trouble and should not be afraid to show our love practically.

9   What About the Children?

On October 30th, 1990, Polly Toynbee, writing in the *Independent* newspaper said, 'The research pours out showing that the children of divorce tend to do badly in terms of health, education, and happiness. The effects last into later life and they are more likely to suffer depression, commit suicide, die in accidents, drink heavily, take worse jobs than their peers and get divorced.'

Visit any criminal court in the land on any day of the week and you will see how true this is. Even though the social enquiry reports are not read out publicly, time and time again it is quite clear to all that the person in the dock is partly there because of a faulty start in life. A typical court report would read:

> Joe Bloggs was born in London in 1972. Shortly after his birth, his parents separated for ten months until they became reconciled for two stormy years until 1974 when his sister (now adopted) was born. In 1978 when he was six, after witnessing several serious acts of violence between his parents, he was taken to live with his grand-mother. This proved successful until she died in 1984, three days before his twelfth birthday. By then his mother, now an alcoholic, had moved away and his father was nowhere to be found . . .

Is it any wonder that the child concerned found it hard to grow up a decent citizen?

Mercifully, many do. Furthermore, although much modern thinking is against this, we are all responsible for our actions. It is not good enough to put all the blame on our parents or lack of parents. These factors should be taken into consideration but, if we are to have any human dignity at all, we must be responsible for our own actions.

We should never forget that when people divorce, a child can be deprived and neglected although materially rich. Divorce is no respecter of social background. Its effects are less immediately apparent when the parents are comfortably off but they are just as real to the 'poor little rich girl' or 'poor little rich boy'.

Children first

Faced with these facts, any parent, particularly a Christian parent, should feel very concerned about divorce. But this book will have no purpose at all if it does not attempt to help and encourage those facing such problems. Frankly it will be a damage limitation exercise; some damage is inevitable but we can limit it – we must limit it and God will help us.

So, now that divorce has begun, what can we do as parents and helpers? The answer is a good deal.

How can the parent help?

Underlying all, we must remember that the children are the priority. Their welfare is paramount. Now, by saying this, I am not suggesting that they should be the centre of attention, the heroes of a sordid drama, all eyes upon them. I would advocate the opposite. Far too many parents tell their children far too much. It may give the parents temporary relief but it can do the children permanent harm. None the less, quietly and lovingly, they should be considered all the time. Logically, this means that if their interests were truly considered, the parents wouldn't divorce at all. By continuing their behaviour, they have firmly put their interests before those of the children. But, realistically, I'll assume that divorce is inevitable.

Telling them straight

The aim of both parties, whatever their conduct and whatever their feelings towards each other, should be that the children should have a good relationship throughout their lives, with both parents. Therefore, even if mother has committed adultery and put her own pleasure before her duty as wife and mother, or even if father has continually drunk to excess, well knowing that this would ruin the marriage, she is still the children's mother and he is still the children's father. Furthermore, except in rare circumstances, she is still the best mother for the child and he is still the best father. There are exceptions, but generally an 'imperfect mother' is better for a child than a 'perfect foster mother'. Without wishing to attack the social welfare authorities (who face enormous problems, with very difficult cases and very little funds), I must say it is very sad indeed when children are not brought up in a family atmosphere, preferably their own.

In December 1992, the Jubilee Policy Group, a Christian organisation based in Cambridge, published *Relational Justice, A New Approach to Penal Reform*. With Home Office approval, 358 prisoners in 20 prisons were interviewed in the summer of 1992; of the 330 men, 29 per cent had been in care as children.

So, parents, whatever their feelings to each other, should try to have their children living with one or other of them and should try to assist their children to have a good relationship with both. This can be particularly hard on a Christian parent where the other parent is wilfully leading a non-Christian life. We know from Exodus 20:12, the fifth commandment, 'Honour your father and your mother, that your days may be long in the land which the Lord your God gives you.' How can this be reconciled with the adulterous mother or the violent father? I don't know the complete answer but I suggest that, without condoning the conduct of the other parent, Christians can honestly say to their children, 'Well, I know that Dad's difficult when he has had too much to drink but he is your dad. He loves you very much and you must try to do what he says – when he is sober.' We just have to trust God and go on praying when our children are living with a non-Christian parent.

Early on, in order to lay the foundations of a good relationship, ideally both parents should tell the children the truth – commensurate with their ability to understand.

This is difficult, very difficult and particularly hard for the guilty party but, if they have any decency left, they should try. The younger the children, the vaguer the details. You shouldn't lie but there is no point in telling them the unsavoury details. Better to say, 'My loves, you know Mummy and I haven't been happy for a long time. Well, we are going to live in different houses. Mummy is going to look after you and I am going to see you every weekend and we will have fun.' These words sound hollow and trite; indeed, they are, because in a real sense the children have been betrayed by their parents. But it's the best you can do. As the children get older, or if they are older already, you can fill in the details but no more than is necessary. There is no point in getting at the other party under the pretext of 'telling the children the truth'. Incidentally, the truth will out anyway. If you are 'innocent', you don't have to justify yourself. If you are 'guilty', you can't justify yourself. Let time and truth provide the answer gradually. Christians should particularly beware of making moral statements, correct though they may be, solely for the purpose of getting at the other parent.

Whether you decide to tell the children alone or together, try to be as objective and fair as possible. This is tough, particularly if you are on the receiving end of the divorce. However, it can be done. A useful trick is to imagine yourself as 'a fly on the wall'. Would that fly, overhearing what has been said, consider it was being said fairly, with as little stress and tension as possible?

Parental role

Your next ambition should be to remain a parent, not a pal, to your children and to help the other parent retain some parental dignity. God is our Father. We are his children. He is, praise be, our friend as well, but he is primarily our Father. We should treat him with respect, even though he loves us and we love him. We earthly parents should have this role model well in mind.

We must remain parents and in a sense we must keep our distance and help the other parent to do the same. Now, I am not suggesting the Victorian image of papa seen for half an hour after tea. I am all for bathing the children, changing the nappies, cutting the grass and all that. All the same, we are parents. We should never forget it. The breakdown of parental responsibility, the way in which many parents have opted out of their responsibilities, is one of the main causes of society's problems today. Such parents are equipping their children very badly for later life.

So, as parents, we must not spoil our children. We didn't when we were living with them and we shouldn't when we are apart from them. Naturally, if we only have access once a week, we will give them a better tea. But, don't overdo it. Those who attempt to buy the children's love by spoiling them are doing the children great harm even if, temporarily at least, it appears to work. It is emotional blackmail and as an old High Court judge once said, blackmail is sometimes worse than murder.

If the other parent is trying to buy the children's affection, away from you, and this happens all too often, what can you do? Sometimes very little. But, in my experience, if you love them and understand them they will usually stick by you particularly if you remember to make life enjoyable. Helping them make a cake and then ice it followed by a borrowed video of *Tom and Jerry* can work wonders. Children are often far shrewder and more loyal than we realise. In short, your influence over and your effect upon the children is much more dependent on your loving relationship with them than on the time and money you spend on them. Mind you, this is always provided that you aren't spending all your time and money on horses and drink!

Don't make it difficult

Access (the new in-word is 'contact' but it means access) is as easy or as difficult as you, the parents, make it. Thousands of parents handle it with care and common sense, oiled by humour. The problems are minimal. On the other hand, a few parents make it as difficult and nasty as they possibly can. You can see more unpleasantness, more naked hate in custody/access disputes than on many a battlefield. It is a battlefield, the parents working out their bitter hatred of each other, using the children as pawns, inflicting incalculable damage upon them. Beware of getting into such a situation because it can escalate out of all proportion. Sometimes, only one party is really to blame but it often takes two.

As Christians, we know that we have to forgive again and again and again. Seventy times seven. Even non-Christians must see that the less bitter they are towards their former spouse the more chance there is of establishing a working relationship over the children. So, the sooner you start to forgive and forget the better, even during the trauma of the actual divorce.

Flexibility should be your aim. You were flexible when you were happily married. Why not be flexible now that you are not? In other words, don't be too rigid. If she wants to alter that weekend because her cousin has suddenly come from Australia, agree. If he wants to take your son to football because of a sudden spare ticket, let him. And so what if, from time to time, the children come home a little late or a little dirty? Such tolerance can be abused and limits may have to be set but, generally, an easy to and fro is much better than rigid guidelines. The older the children, the more the flexibility.

The right of access

Two important points are worth noting here. First, if at all possible, try to live close by. I am eternally grateful to my two older children, then aged ten and eight, for asking me to move back to Chiswick, where they lived with their mother in my former home, when I had moved to Fulham intending to remain there. As they put it, 'It will be much easier for us, Daddy.' Although painful at the time, in the end it has been well worth doing, such that now some eleven years later we are all still in Chiswick. Happily married, I now have three young children and the older ones visit as the whim takes them. In some instances, this cannot be done and some parents who have the custody of the children have deliberately moved, sometimes abroad, in order to thwart the relationship with the other parent. Generally, you can live close by, even if it means rejecting that good job offer, tempting though Hong Kong may be before 1997.

Second, and I well remember the pain, try and keep up access however hard it is for you. After all, seeing your children in your home with the lover in your dressing-gown at your table with your wife is pain indeed. But the pain will pass and the children need you. Access is *their* right, not yours. As Lord Justice Elizabeth Butler-Sloss, who chaired the Cleveland enquiry, said in autumn 1990, 'It is the children's right, not the right of the parent, to have a continuing relationship with the non-custodial parent.'

This requires courage. I have never forgotten an admirable man, so distressed by his wife's adultery that he refused ever again to see their two sons because of the pain it caused him. This may be quite understandable, but

the sons needed him and he was a good man in a responsible position with much to offer them. The moral is
persevere.

Incidentally, during access visits or after access visits,
never pump the children for information about the other
parent. 'I see that Mummy's got a new car.' 'Did you like
Daddy's new girlfriend?' It is not right. However subtly
done, the children will see through your questions and be
hurt by them. How much should they tell you? Are they
being disloyal to Dad? Didn't Mum say not to tell about
Arthur? The children will tell you what they want to tell
you. It is not fair to probe. What is more, your job is to
build up your own self-esteem. You won't do this by looking over your shoulder at the past. Concentrate, with
God's help, on your present and your future and that of
your children. For years I didn't follow this advice,
thereby hurting myself and confusing my children.

Finally, stress that divorce is not their fault. Apparently
many children feel that their parents broke up because
they were 'naughty' or 'expensive' or whatever. All children need the reassurance that they are not to blame. It
is terrible to think that they should have to carry this
burden when they have burdens enough anyway. They
may well not say this, knowing that this would hurt and
anger you. You may well have to get them to spill the
beans, possibly to a close friend or a wise grandparent or
godparent. It is the thorn which must be pulled out as
quickly and painlessly as possible.

How can the helper help?

One of the duties of the advocate, solicitor or barrister,
is to assimilate the facts and law of a case and feed them
in palatable form to the judge and, sometimes, the jury.
'All judges are perfect but some are more perfect than
others.' Thus, if you have a quick-witted judge your sub-
mission can be pithy. Alternatively, if you have an old
stickler (and there are still a few), you will have to adjust

your submissions accordingly. It is a case of horses for courses.

The helper faced with the victim should do likewise. Nothing will be gained by being dominant or bossy. The parent is vulnerable, so are the children, and it is all too easy for those of us who are not emotionally involved to offer advice. By all means do, but cautiously and lovingly or not at all. You may find it useful to listen to various tapes and read various books, perhaps making some notes of your own. Once you have fully digested the contents, then and only then can you gently spoon-feed them to those who need help. My father-in-law is masterly at this. Drawing on his pipe, he'll begin by saying, 'We were just wondering . . .' or 'I have been thinking over that problem . . .' Wise, pertinent advice then follows, but so graciously that we listen and usually follow it.

Furthermore, many people faced with a splitting marriage among their friends just cannot cope at all. They should cope but they can't cope. If so, and you cannot face either of the parents, could you not at least consider the children and face them? They are innocent and they do need you.

Your own children can help too

What is more, your own children can help too. It is good for children to appreciate their own good fortune and that we should, all of us, young or old, lovingly serve one another. In a real sense, Christians are one family. Your four-year-old can have a child to tea. Our young children did so recently when a young mother died of cancer. Our seven-year-old, Harriet, inspired by the children's TV programme 'Blue Peter', ran a bring-and-buy sale for the blind people in Africa and raised three hundred pounds. Your fourteen-year-old can be asked, or even told, to take someone on a bike ride or for a swim.

Include the children on treats but make the treats as normal and natural as possible. Don't patronise, don't overwhelm. The victim parent is very vulnerable, very sensitive. They don't want charity but they do need help, particularly for their children. So, why not invite the child to join you for a day at the seaside (which incidentally gives mum a break) or your visit to the local cinema with supper afterwards? Be inclusive. The local church can help greatly, but informal treats are probably the best of all.

Standing in

You can stand in for the missing parent. So, if you are good at football why not ask young Tom to join your son in a kickabout? If you are near a deserted father with two young girls why not ask them round to help make the cakes for the school play? The feminists may dislike these stereotypes but I am unrepentant. The child needs both parents. We can, within limits, be role models.

Some years ago, a friend gave tea to two children whose mother had suddenly died and whose father did not come home each night until about six o'clock. For many months, she calmly and quietly bridged a vulnerable gap. Again, I think of a deserted mother who arrived at our church with three young children. The youngest, a boy of about five, was particularly active and lively. He had a young godfather, in his early twenties. Week in, week out, this young godfather took on a role somewhere between father and big brother to the immense benefit of the little boy. And, incidentally, to himself now that he has a child of his own.

The role of grandparents

The older generation have much to offer. One of the saddest truths in divorce is that not only does the child lose, or partly lose, a parent but, so often, the grandparents on the losing side are even more pushed out of the picture. 'Oh, I haven't seen my grandchildren for years ever since my son divorced and she went up north.' How often does one hear this? If older, we can help the children. We can pray for them. We have the time. Many parents don't.

We can remember them on their birthday and Christmas.
We can send them postcards on holiday. We can go to
their school functions. It need not cost much but the
rewards are high. Indeed, many an old person has ben-
efited enormously. Our little children have a loyal and
devoted friend, Elspeth, now nearer ninety than eighty.
They exchange letters and, on the rare occasions when
they go to lunch, it is sheer delight to hear solemn dis-
cussions between them on the relative merits of marma-
lade and Marmite sandwiches or other such burning topics
of the day. Our former cleaner, Dolly, has a similarly rich
relationship, arriving for tea, armed with sweet biscuits
and racy information about all the neighbourhood. They
are both valued honorary great aunts, although this title
has a depressingly solemn ring about it.

. All this presupposes that the parent welcomes such
help. Some do not.

You can help with money. Expense can be minimal,
but it need not be. As we all know, divorce is costly for
all concerned and very often the parent with the children
is struggling to make ends meet on a limited and uncertain
budget. Instead of an anonymous donation to a charity,
why not consider the problem on your doorstep? Cash
may well be embarrassing, so perhaps you can help in
kind. Well worth doing. Although you want to help, perhaps in gratitude for your own happy family life or because
you yourself have now recovered from an unhappy time,
you may not actually know of any particularly deserving
cause. Look around or ask. At this very moment, I can
think of parents and children who are in deep trouble,
practically and emotionally, let alone spiritually. Wher-
ever you are, people need help. I learnt recently of a man
who 'had so much money he didn't know what to do with
it'. This remark still rankles, considering the difficulties
so many people face. Alternatively, if there really are no
needy cases in your neighbourhood then a contribution to
a national charity is always welcome.

Nearer home, some parents with children to entertain

on access visits have no suitable home to which to take them. Walking around the park in a hail-storm is not much fun. You have a house; why not lend it? Only those of us who have lived with our family in a family house and then lost it can fully understand this. I make no apologies for repeating this point. All your heart and probably all your money and all your possessions, except your toothbrush, are in that house and not only are you effectively banned from it but you may well have the additional pain of knowing that somebody, quite improperly, is living in it. Saturday comes. The children are dropped outside your bedsitter. What are you to do with them? The friend who picks you up and lends his home is a friend indeed. If those friends, having given you all lunch, can then leave you alone with the children until after tea, so much the better.

There are official access centres. In many ways, they are admirable, filling an undoubted gap, but they are institutional and are often overcrowded, with limited opening hours. A private home is better.

Absent parents

Finally, when you are with the children, it sometimes helps to mention the absent parent, but not to criticise and not obtrusively. To over-mention is as damaging as to under-mention. But such a phrase as, 'I first met your daddy fishing, do you like fishing?' can help rebuild the damaged image in the child's mind. At home, daddy may not be mentioned at all. Always refer to 'mummy' or 'daddy' or 'mum' or 'dad'; 'your mother' or 'your father' is chillingly formal.

Reread Isaiah 61 and 'comfort all who mourn . . . give them a garland instead of ashes.'

These words may seem light-years away from drinking lukewarm tea out of a chipped cup with a weeping friend in a railway buffet. We are servants of God and, as such, required to bring his love where it is most needed. The

Holy Spirit will give us the courage and energy and insight to do what is right. He will inspire us. Our contribution may seem very menial, even trivial or silly, but it is all part of God's plan to bind up the broken-hearted and restore them to health and happiness.

AFTER A DIVORCE

10 Tying Up Loose Ends

The decree has been made absolute. You have obtained your divorce. Legally the matter is settled, but emotionally there is still much work to be done. Indeed, in many ways, the decree absolute is irrelevant and it is almost always an anticlimax. The essential point to grasp is that unless yours was a short marriage with no children, in a sense a divorce is never final. As I have said before, it is not an event, it is a process.

Whether or not you had children, the longer the marriage, the longer will be the aftermath. Your families, your friends, even your acquaintances, will be intermingled. Untangling takes time; the more carefully it is done, the better for your future happiness.

A dignified exit

If you do have children your responsibilities towards them will continue or, at least, should continue until your death. However, these responsibilities do change over the years. When our children have finished their full-time education, we are responsible for them although, naturally, our relationship will alter with the years. Likewise, as we get older, our children may have to be responsible for us. It is a two-way traffic of mutual support and encouragement based on love. The parent/child relationship may well be very damaged by divorce but it shouldn't sever. Again, how we handle matters now, just after divorce, will affect our relationship with our children and our grandchildren for many years to come.

In short, recovery from a divorce is a process and your attitude is crucial. Selwyn Hughes, the well-known Christian writer, usefully tells an instructive tale of two young women who were widowed. One was emotionally crippled as a result of her experiences and spent the rest of her life unhappy and causing unhappiness. She was embittered, only considering herself. The other, having worked through her grief, devoted the rest of her life to loving and helping others. The external facts were similar; their inner reactions totally different.

St Paul in 1 Corinthians 9:24 talks of runners. Quite a useful picture is to envisage athletes running in a race, passing the finishing line yet continuing to run for quite a distance before they walk and ultimately rest altogether. It would harm them if they stopped dead just past the finishing line. Likewise, during our divorce, our energies and those of our family and friends have been all geared up to the decree absolute, the finishing line. But we should still continue to run for a little while, as should our helpers, because there is still work to be done.

Another analogy may assist. Reverting to the picture of the marriage as a house, the house has now been demolished by divorce. The site has still to be cleared. You can either have an ugly bombsite, with weeds, rubble and craters, which can harm you and others. Or, you can level the site, putting down stone or gravel which require minimum maintenance.

Living in London, I pass derelict buildings nearly every day, their walls covered with graffiti, their windows gaping, their gardens a mass of bottles, cans and weeds. These buildings are an intrinsic danger. If you enter them you could get hurt, even killed. But once the site is landscaped, not only is the danger removed but the whole townscape is improved. These analogies obviously mustn't be taken too far, but I have found them quite useful both for myself and for others.

Don't look back

In Isaiah 43:18–19 we read, 'Remember not the former things; nor consider the things of old. Behold, I am doing a new thing; now it springs forth, do you not perceive it?' The key is to forget the former things. Emotional spring-cleaning is required. You must learn to let go of the past, always remembering that your former partner is no longer your property or your problem. Of course, particularly if you have children, you may have to have some dealings together but you must sever the emotional tie. Not easy; some people never do it but, on the assumption that most of us who are divorced do so before middle age, do remember that we should have another thirty or forty years of life to live. Far better to live those years in the present, looking to the future, than being trapped in the past, an ever-receding past.

When married, you were one flesh. Now you are not. It is essential you learn to lead an independent life. You must try not to be hurt by the successes or delighted by the failures of your former partner. Few, if any of us, live up to this perfection but, for our own health and happiness, we should certainly try to do so. Most people know the story of Lot's wife turning into a pillar of salt as she fled from Sodom and Gomorrah (Genesis 19:26). Why was she turned into a pillar of salt? Because she looked back. And if we continue to look back, metaphorically, we are in danger of the same fate befalling us. Mothers trapped with children understandably find it very hard.

Another picture is of those old-fashioned gramophones where the needle had a tendency to stick in the groove, endlessly repeating itself: '. . . and then I found the letter in her handbag' – 'after that I was in hospital for eight days' – '. . . and he never even remembered Tom's birthday'. Please don't get stuck in these grooves. It is not healthy for you or for others.

To help avoid this it is as well to trim as many loose ends as possible. Some people, whether consciously or not, prolong the aftermath of a divorce, endlessly finding problems which necessitate contact with the other side. Thus, even ten years after a divorce, solicitors may still be investigating the small print of a time-share agreement or the ultimate destination of the piano. If you possibly can, don't do this. Far better to have a clean break, even if this means that you have to concede points rather than protract proceedings. On a basic note, better to let her have the piano than spend hundreds of pounds over many years haggling over ownership. In short, you should 'clear the decks', always remembering that if you have not sorted out old issues with your parents or your previous partners you are all the more likely to find yourself entrapped in similar conflicts in your new relationships.

On a personal note, only a few weeks ago, while sorting out my desk, I found a letter which could have reopened an issue with my former wife from whom I have been divorced for over eleven years. We now get on well. I just threw the letter in the waste-paper basket. This attitude undoubtedly pays. A few weeks later, she came round with some books and toys from our former home in case they were of use. That apart, learn to let go. Even if you never meet again, be reconciled in your own mind.

More about children

This attitude should also prevail with the children. They have been through the storm and we should consider them a major priority, our aim being to re-establish them in a loving relationship with both parents. We should try to establish a flexible pattern. Normally, parents are admirably sensible and, quite rightly, work these matters out without the assistance of lawyers and the courts. It is trite but true to point out that an informal decision worked out by parents is almost bound to be better than any formal legal decision. You cannot legislate for the vagaries of human nature so even the best court order is inferior to sensible, parental agreement. The judge may well be learned in the law, possibly quite wise. But it is *your* family and, unless your former partner is quite impossible (as they sometimes are), you should be able to work out the day-to-day details yourselves. What is more, if there are some difficulties, make certain that you are advised by fair-minded family, friends or solicitors. It is not unknown for delicate situations to be worsened by lawyers whose whole attitude seems dominated by scoring points against the other side and increasing their fees.

Flexibility, tolerance, give and take are what matter. If he brings the children back half an hour late from time to time, so what? If she alters the weekend rather late in the day (and she was always like this) so what? The happiness of the children is what matters rather than your temporary inconvenience. Of course, if such tolerance is abused then you may have to go to law and, with some difficult parents, the sooner firm boundaries are defined, the better. But, on the whole, sort it out yourself.

Concerning access, the older the children, the more the choice is theirs until, as teenagers, their decision is final. At this time, particularly if the children are living away from you, try to keep up access to them if this is what they want, however painful it may be. This needs restating because if you let access lapse at this crucial time and then try to restore it many months later, you will find it very difficult, perhaps impossible, and both you and your children will be the losers.

A plea to older children
Let me say at this point a word to older children directly. When your parents first divorce it is not surprising that, because they are in difficulties, they may well say things about the other parent which should not be said. One or both of your parents' may have behaved very badly. All

the same, try hard to form your own independent relationship with each of your parents. Your parents' quarrels are not your quarrels. The Bible tells you to honour your father and mother.

I recently read in a magazine a corrosive article by a young woman whose parents' marriage had recently failed. In it she stated that she intended to have nothing further to do with her father who had run off with somebody else. I don't know all the facts but I question whether this attitude will ultimately do either her, her mother or her father any good. And, when she comes to marry, what about her husband and her own children? This is not the long-term solution.

Don't outlaw the in-laws!

Talking to parents again: as far as possible, try to rebuild links with your in-laws. If they have been the villains of the piece, in your mind, this may not be easy. But, very often, the grandparents have been most distressed by the divorce and should be forgiven if, from time to time, they have overreacted or have supported their own child against you. After all, you and I would probably do the same. Now that you are divorced remember the difficulties they faced and also remember that, probably, they heard only one side of the truth. It is far better to re-establish contact with them, if you have children. If you do not have children, this may not be necessary.

So often, grandparents have an affinity with their grandchildren which is lacking between parent and child. Grandparents often have the time and the wisdom which we parents lack. Genetically, half of our child's heritage comes from each side. In fact, one side may well turn out to be more dominant than the other. Thus, your husband's father may well have more to offer your son than your own father just because he likes fishing whereas your father prefers books. For your children's sake, foster this relationship, see that they remember birthdays and

Christmases and encourage visits and telephone calls, even if, for a while, you find it too painful to be closely involved.

The same principles should apply to certain valuable old friends, though you may rightly decide that some friendships are beyond recall. From your point of view, this may be true, but not necessarily from your children's. Unless you consider the friendship undesirable, it may be as well to continue it, even on a less intense level, for the sake of your children. As for yourself, you have many years in which to forge new friendships. One can still make friends after the age of thirty. Since becoming a committed Christian in my early forties, I have discovered that one of the greatest joys of the Christian life is transcending so many barriers of age, type and class which, in the outside world, pathetically limit one's friends to a very small circle. With God our Father, we are all brothers and sisters.

Challenges

Now is the time to get involved generously in challenges which will take you out of yourself. During the divorce, you probably lacked the time, the will and the energy to do this. Summon up your willpower, take your courage in both hands and attempt something different, even difficult. It is not a question of money, which may well be in very short supply. It is far more a question of confidently looking to the future saying to yourself, 'Well, what have I always wanted to do or see or learn or become?'

I know a woman who faced the death of her two young sons from a wasting disease. She then was divorced and found herself utterly alone. When I met her she was running an old people's home pouring into the old people all the love and energy that she had. A remarkable achievement.

Alex Torbet is a murderer serving a life sentence at Saughton prison, Edinburgh. His advice is being sought by scientists and academics the world over because he has become internationally known for his ability to breed fish. Apparently his work could play a part in freeing people in the Third World from hunger.

These examples make the point that people faced with almost overwhelming problems can, with courage, triumphantly overcome them.

Some years ago, the flavour of the month was Canadian army exercises. The idea was that, whatever your age and health, if you practised them eleven minutes a day, your health would radically improve. Many of us tried, only to fall by the wayside a few weeks later. But the principle was undoubtedly correct. Every day, you exercise. Every day, little by little you become healthier. Likewise with forgiveness, so forgive daily. Practise each day.

Forgiveness is a decision not a feeling. Let me repeat that. Forgiveness is a decision not a feeling. It is an act of will. You *decide* to forgive. Here a little, there a little. Begin with small gestures, begin by forgiving small things, gradually moving to the fundamentals. Remember St Paul in Romans 3:22–3 tells us 'there is no distinction; since all have sinned and fall short of the glory of God'. This includes you, even if you have much to forgive.

In plain human terms, whatever your religious beliefs, remember that if you continue to blame your former spouse for your troubles this will stop you from rebuilding your own life. You will continue to feel like a victim and you will be letting your past taint your present and your future. Without doubt, in these difficult times, we need God's help and, already, we may well have to pray to be able to forgive at all. Your aim should be to be reconciled with your partner. By this, I do not mean reconciliation by returning to live together (though it would be wonderful if this were to take place). What is intended is a feeling of reconciliation such that you no longer harbour any bitterness. For many years after my divorce, when I was praying for my former wife and those involved with her, I used to pray for them 'in brackets' until one happy day I just removed the brackets and prayed for them like anyone else – it was a great release.

Only when all these matters have been substantially settled, should you consider a new deep relationship.

How to help

What about the helpers? Are they still needed or can they gracefully retire? Without doubt, they are still needed and, in many ways, their help may well be more important now than before. The reason is that when a divorce is going through everyone is keyed up, well aware that 'Jane's divorce is coming up in March' or 'Tom's sorting the money out in April.' At that time, the victim not only has personal help but also professional help which, if the matter has been going on for a long time, may well also verge on the personal. In short, the divorce has a high profile and then, with decree absolute, comes anticlimax and there is an understandable tendency on the part of the helper to consider that the job is done. But it isn't. The victims may well be less vocal about their problems. There may well be less involvement with the other side or with lawyers and the courts. But they are still in a most vulnerable position and still need your help, even if it is hard for them to ask for it.

Let me put it like this. In the early days, when there was a custody hearing, quite understandably a worried parent might well ask you to come along to give moral support. So, you would reschedule your diary and go. Six months later, although there is no court hearing, the same parent is still very anxious about seeing or not seeing the children and still wants to talk over problems with you. They may well not ask, so you will just have to telephone or drop by just to 'see how things are'.

The reality is that the victim, whether husband or wife, is older, battle-scarred, and still convalescent. Practically speaking, their circumstances may well have changed radically. A few years ago, a man on a good income might have been living in a nice house, with two cars and three children. Now, having missed promotion, he has the same income but more responsibilities: he is living in a small two-bedroomed flat, with a smaller car, enjoying access to two of his children whereas his youngest daughter (wrongly) is being very difficult, thinking the divorce is all his fault. If a woman, it is very likely that she is living in a smaller house, probably in a different place, facing up to the fact that her income has dropped radically. Her children are not all that easy and she is certainly not getting any younger. The first few months, even years, after divorce are very tough and the future happiness of both parent and child may well be determined by what happens in this period of transition.

As helpers, we should be discreetly in the wings. It would be unwise, even impertinent, to be too closely involved because people must learn to stand on their own feet, unless there are exceptional circumstances. On the other hand, if you are not involved at all, the victim may well feel even more deserted than ever. So keep praying and gently keep on helping as you did during the early stages of divorce.

Easier for men

It has to be faced that life for a man under these circumstances is almost always easier than for a woman. Usually the mother has the custody of the children so her social life is considerably restricted. Furthermore, she may well have missed working for many years and, when seeking employment, she may well find that she has to be retrained. What is more, she will have the perennial problem of who is to keep an eye on the children now that her husband is not available. Whatever the background, these problems are very hard to handle.

The man, on the other hand, is considerably freer. He does not have the daily pains and pleasures of his children. He has probably worked throughout the marriage and even if his career has suffered he is still capable of earning his living. Furthermore, provided he doesn't sink into self-pity or drink and the like, he will be surprised to find how eligible he is. I am not suggesting that remarriage is an answer to all problems. Far from it. But a single man, with limited family ties, is far more able to rebuild his life than is a woman with dependent children. This is an almost insoluble problem and all of us, whether Christians or not, should try to mitigate its harsh effects as far as we possibly can.

11 New Relationships – Remarriage?

Statistics have been likened to a drunkard leaning against a lamppost in that they are often used for support rather than illumination. Apparently second marriages have a less-than-30 per cent chance of surviving five years or more whereas third marriages have a less-than-15 per cent chance of surviving five years or more. Whether or not you accept the validity of these figures matters little. What is quite clear is that remarriage is not a soft option and, unless handled with care, can well lead to tears.

A tale of two marriages

Let me begin with two friends whose stories are true and have much to teach us. Both married comparatively young, both had children. Both marriages ended against their wishes. They were very upset, as were their children but, all in all, they had behaved with reasonable dignity and common sense. The future was relatively hopeful.

Then, their paths began to diverge and, many years later, the seeds sown in those early post-divorce years have grown into mature plants. One friend was determined that no serious new relationship would be considered let alone started until as many as possible of the loose ends of the first had been tidied up. Thus, strenuous efforts were made to tie up the finances, to sell the house, to resettle the children, fixing such matters as access and maintenance, the whole idea being to make as clean a break as possible.

Conversely, the other friend, against all rhyme or reason, embarked on a new intense relationship even before the divorce was finalised and before any of the loose ends were tied up at all. The matrimonial home was not yet sold, the maintenance was not yet sorted out, the children were still deeply unsettled when the friend and his new partner decided to live together only a few miles down the road.

The result? Inevitably, the first friend fared much better than the second. In the first case, after the divorce a reasonable, even friendly, relationship was established between all concerned, to the considerable benefit of the children. When this friend later remarried, everyone co-operated. As to the other, the wrangling continues to this day. One painful result is that the children of the first marriage have never seen, let alone become friendly with, the children of the second marriage. How very sad. Particularly if we remarry later in life, our children have all the more need of their older half-brothers and sisters.

I am still in close contact with both of these friends, their former families and their new families. Moreover, as you no doubt have found, if you yourself are divorced, people tend to share their own experiences with you. Thus, certain common points emerge which are well worth considering.

Take it slowly

The first principle is, don't rush. Don't rush into another relationship before you have recovered from the trauma of the first. Perhaps this analogy may help: every year in the London marathon many runners, both amateur and professional, run through London, raising money for charity. The event has become increasingly popular. You have to be fit to run in a race and very fit indeed to run in a marathon. You have to train, controlling your food and drink and exercising regularly. If you don't, not only would you not complete the marathon but you might damage your health, even fatally. Marriage is a marathon. In our first marathon, whether our fault or not, we stumbled and fell. We needed doctors and nurses to patch us up and, even now, have not fully regained our former fitness. How silly to enter another marathon before we've recovered from the first.

Another way of looking at it is to consider scar tissue. Your divorce has left you with scar tissue and you must let this heal properly otherwise there is a high chance that you will knock the scab off the wound or wounds and the whole healing process will have to start all over again. (I trust doctors will forgive me if, medically, these details are not quite correct!) The point is that emotionally, you must let your emotional wounds heal, working through the grief process until you feel strong again. This is a counsel of perfection which few of us can attain. Right at the end, a new relationship can of course complete the recovery, but try to recover as much as you can before undertaking this new relationship.

In practical terms, this entails sorting out as many residual problems as you can. Loose ends, like flaying ropes on board ship, can trip you. These loose ends may not be directly connected with your former marriage. They may also entail your getting your private finances, as far as possible, into a more healthy shape. Likewise, your health. While going through a divorce, you may have started to drink too much or have started smoking to excess. Now is the time to tackle these problems. In short, you must attempt to put your house in order.

Living with who you are

Leading from this, we come to a second important principle which is learning to live with yourself. George Bernard Shaw once said that the one golden rule is that there are no golden rules. I disagree. Before you consider a new relationship, leading to remarriage, the golden rule is that you must learn to live with yourself, as an independent individual under God. I found this very hard to do. Going from boarding-school to university to sharing digs in London, followed by ten years of happy marriage, I was singularly ill-equipped to live on my own. Over forty, I found that my friends were nearly all married. I hadn't had to cook or wash or iron for many years, not that I hadn't pulled my weight in my first marriage because, in fairness to myself, I consider that I had. All the same, the temptation to avoid some of these problems, both practical and emotional, by living with somebody else was very strong indeed.

I am so glad that I did not. With hindsight, I find it was very valuable indeed to have the time and opportunity to work out or attempt to work out where I was going. Most of us, once launched on marriage and our career, never stop to give ourselves time to think. We save this up for retirement which is often far too late. As the poet W. H. Davies so well puts it, 'What is this life if, full of care, we have no time to stand and stare.' Once you can live with yourself, warts and all, you stand a very much better chance of living successfully with somebody else. As a Christian, you are never alone. You are loved by God as an individual, in your own right, whatever your past and your problems. Furthermore, if you are blessed as I was by a supportive family and by an active, loving Christian community, your loneliness is much less than for many in the outside world.

Was it Don Juan who said that marriage is like a besieged city? Those married inside it want to get out whereas those outside it want to get in. Many single people imagine that if only they were married their problems would disappear overnight. How very wrong they are. There is considerable pressure in being married. Personally, I consider that the married state is the answer, but the joys of being single should not be forgotten. To have complete control of one's money, one's time, one's life is not to be sneezed at, even allowing for periods of loneliness and frustration. These are all matters which deserve serious consideration as you learn to live with yourself.

Once you are through this transitional period and have decided that you would like to settle down again with somebody else, may I suggest that you take into account some points which, in the happy heat of the moment, you may well overlook.

The effects of age

An obvious point. Your potential new partner is very likely to be older than your first. This partner could be older and wiser; if so, so much the better. On the other hand, life may well have taken its toll. Our experiences affect us. As Christians we know that we can lay these painful experiences at the foot of the Cross, seek forgiveness, receive forgiveness and start again, but such is human nature, we often do not do this. There are areas of sin in dirty, dusty corners of our house which fester away with the result that when we contemplate remarriage, we are more tarnished than we were in our twenties. We are more tarnished and so is our potential partner.

In addition, being older, we will both lack the youthful resilience, the sheer energy, which, in the early days of our first marriage, just carried us through problems, at least for a while. So, objectively, as far as you can be objective in the affairs of the heart, it is a good idea to examine yourself and each other before the matter gets too serious.

The effects of children

Children and stepchildren are considered in the following chapter. Remember that one of the main causes of failure or difficulty in remarriages is the effect of the children. Children almost always remain loyal to their own parents and will, time and time again, cause trouble for stepparents. It is only natural for us to feel more close to our own children than others'. If you are going to set up a home, both of you bringing children to the family, there may well be conflicts of loyalty. These conflicts can be resolved but it is glib thinking not to anticipate them before you embark on a new relationship. Furthermore, never underestimate the trouble which older children can cause. Whatever their ages, some children can be plain difficult once their parents seek to remarry, even if the parents divorced many years before and even if the parent is seeking to marry somebody totally unconnected with the breakdown of the first marriage. On one view, these children, once they have left the nest, should consider that their parents' lives are no concern of theirs. On the other hand, our parents are always our parents and, particularly if we are rather vulnerable ourselves, we can be disturbed by new relationships even if adults ourselves.

I can think of at least one instance when a child, grown-up and professionally qualified, determined to make the parent's new marriage founder. The effort failed but not before considerable lasting damage had been done.

Needless to say, these points are not meant to alarm you. They are just worth considering as is the status of the person you are thinking of marrying.

If single

If your new partner has not been married before, they may well not be used to the hurly-burly of family life. By rule of thumb, the happier a childhood enjoyed, with the benefit of brothers and sisters, the less of a problem in later life. All the same, your intended partner may have had no real intimate contact with children whatsoever and will, quite justifiably, lack that rapport or touch with children which most of us have, to some extent, once we have children of our own. If this is so, there is all the more reason to take the relationship slowly and very slowly indeed with your children. They have lost their father so they may well find a potential stepfather very threatening. They may well misbehave and he, in turn, will be

uncertain of how to react. Does he take such misbehaviour seriously or does he attempt to laugh it off? If he
had children of his own he would probably instinctively
know which course of action was better.

Years ago, in the grand days of Hollywood, I enjoyed
a film which explored this problem. The father fell in love
with a beautiful younger woman. His children quite deliberately put her through her paces and, quite convincingly,
showed the father that she was quite unsuited to family
life. Being Hollywood he promptly reunited with his wife
and they all lived happily ever after! While some childless
people have an innate ability to get on with children,
some, nice as they are, just can't get it right.

If widowed

Your intended partner may have been widowed. The crucial question is, has he or she recovered sufficiently? In
2 Samuel 12:14–23, we can read the moving story of how
God struck down the child that Bathsheba bore to David.
While the child was ill, 'David fasted, and went in and lay
all night upon the ground . . . On the seventh day the
child died . . . Then David arose from the earth, and
washed, and anointed himself, and changed his clothes;
and he went into the House of the Lord, and worshipped;
he then went to his own house; and when he asked they
set food before him and he ate.' Later he said, 'While the
child was still alive, I fasted and wept; for I said, "Who
knows whether the Lord will be gracious to me, that the
child may live?" But now he is dead; why should I fast?
Can I bring him back again? I shall go to him, but he will
not return to me.'

Those widowed should mourn their dead and, if they
wish to remarry, then concentrate on the living. It is vital
that they well and truly bury their dead before contemplating a new relationship. Sadly, some people cannot do this.
They are always harking back, which makes a new
relationship very hard to handle. A variation on this theme

is admirably explored in Daphne du Maurier's novel *Rebecca*. Rebecca, the first wife, is dead but the husband seems haunted by her, thereby seriously endangering his second marriage. Fortunately, once this ghost is exorcised, the second marriage flourishes and the book has a happy ending.

It is unhealthy when people are continually referring to their dead husband or wife, thereby making a new relationship almost impossible. Deep prayer and counselling may well be needed.

At the same time, it is only right that those who marry the widowed should allow some space for memories of the past. It is quite artificial for no mention of the past to be allowed. As with those divorced, the first marriage should be mentioned, quite naturally, from time to time. Moreover, even when you are happily married many years later, there may well be short times when your partner should be allowed privacy for memories. For example, if the first wife or husband died at Christmas, the very festivities may bring back the memories, or the death of parents or particular relatives or friends may well be very poignant. Within limits, they should be allowed to experience these memories in peace. It is all a question of balance.

The past can be very tenacious. I have never forgotten a wedding I attended many years ago. The father of the bride had been dead for over twenty years and the mother had been most happily remarried for many years and had had other children. I know this to be true because I often stayed with them. However, at her daughter's wedding this mother was almost overwhelmed by grief by sudden unexpected memories of the dead father. Mercifully, walking around the graveyard with the sun shining and people laughing, we were able to discuss this so that her family never knew. In fact I am sure that her new husband would have understood.

If divorced

Finally, your new partner may have been divorced. Without suggesting that this book has all the answers, because it plainly hasn't, I would suggest that unless you are reasonably satisfied that your new partner has recovered, you should be cautious. It may well be just a question of time. You may have to say something along the lines of, 'Look, I would love us to become far more deeply involved than we are but, for the moment, I am sure you have got things to sort out so why don't we cool it for a while?' This is easier said than done but if you don't say it you may well have to pay a heavy price later.

Only a few months ago, a Christian friend began to fall for somebody who had not quite recovered from her divorce. It was very painful to see a potentially fruitful relationship end when, who knows, had they waited a little while, something permanent might have come out of it.

In Matthew 7:24–7, Jesus talks of the wise man who built his house upon the rock. 'And the rain fell, and the floods came, and the winds blew and beat upon that house, but it did not fail, because it had been founded on the rock.' A foolish man 'built his house upon the sand; and the rain fell, and the floods came, and the winds blew and beat against that house, and it fell; and great was the fall of it'. The choice is up to you.

12 Stepchildren

Before you read this chapter I recommend that you stop and read the book of Ruth, one of the most beautiful books in the Old Testament. It relates a story from the period of Judges when the world was in a turbulent mess, not unlike today. By contrast, the book of Ruth talks of love and marriage, telling the story of Ruth and her mother-in-law, Naomi. Naomi and her husband, Elimelech of Bethlehem, in a time of famine, went with their two sons to Moab. There Elimelech and his sons died leaving Naomi with her two young daughters-in-law. One, Orpah, left her but Ruth remained alongside Naomi as she returned to Bethlehem saying, 'Entreat me not to leave you or to return from following you; for where you go I will go, and where you lodge I will lodge; your people shall be my people, and your God my God; where you die I will die, and there will I be buried. May the Lord do so to me and more also if even death parts me from you' (1:16–17). The story ends happily in that, with the help of Naomi, Ruth the Moabitess ultimately married Boaz and bore a child for whom Naomi cared. This child became the father of Jesse, the father of King David.

The relationship here was mother-in-law to daughter-in-law, but it provides a loving guide as to how successful such relationships can be. There is no reason why the step-relationship should not be equally fruitful.

Coming to the New Testament, we remember that, while enduring the agony of the Cross, a few moments before he died, Jesus gave the care of his own mother

Mary to John, specifically saying that, thereafter, they should be mother and son (John 19:26–7).

If only we could reach the heights of love epitomised in these relationships! The truth is that, provided we follow certain essential principles, we can achieve very happy relationships with our stepchildren.

I am not a stepfather myself but I have had two stepfathers and a stepmother and am, of course, married to a stepmother, my two children being thirteen and eleven when we married in 1983. Apparently, in 1992 in Great Britain, there were six million people who were part of a step-family. What is more, those very families would be interconnected with other families so you are bound to meet this question, directly or indirectly.

The fundamental message of the Christian gospel is love. God loved us so much that he sent his son Jesus to die on the Cross to pay the penalty for our sins. Moreover, God loves us all equally.

Pulling these words together, how does it help us as step-parents? Considerably. What follows may assist with the practical details but, essentially, difficult though it may be, if we love the mother or father, we should try to love the children.

Dead or alive?

There is an undoubted difference depending on whether the natural parent of your stepchild is alive or dead. No doubt from time to time, you wish it were the latter! There are important adjustments to be made either way. If you marry someone who is widowed you must always respect the children's memories of their dead parent, at the same time making discreet allowance for rose-tinted spectacles. (Indeed, so many 'perfect' people die daily according to their obituaries that I am amazed the world goes on without them.) Seriously, you must accept that you can never replace the dead parent, and the children must always be given space, a niche for that parent's memory and influence.

The older the child, the more the space. Thus, if you take on the child when an infant, your influence will be proportionately greater. Even so, if you are usually called 'Daddy' or 'Mummy', the child should be told the truth when older. If reasonably possible, you should encourage contact with the dead parent's family. They may well have much to contribute both practically and emotionally, particularly if you go on to have a family of your own. Incidentally, while it is useful to find out the truth about the dead parent, it is probably not wise for you, the stepparent, to tell the truth to the child. If home truths have to be told it would be better to persuade someone else to tell them. For example, if the child is saying that his late mother rivalled Mother Theresa in sanctity and you know the truth to be the opposite, try hard not to spill the beans unless absolutely necessary. It will only confuse the child.

Different standards

Generally, the other parent is alive and possibly kicking. It is very difficult when your standards are totally different. You are teetotal whereas Tom's father is alcoholic. You are a Christian whereas Jane's mother is just recovering from her third affair. An insoluble problem, but love, fortified by prayer with humour, can help considerably. When your stepchildren are under your roof, you are entitled to expect them to honour your way of doing things. In short they should respect you and your standards. If they have to be disciplined then their own parents should do this except on rare occasions. At the same time, just as your husband should be scrupulously careful not to be rude about his former wife to the children you should be even more scrupulous.

More optimistically, why not try hard to establish working relationships all round? Believe me, this can be done and, in my own case, I am genuinely grateful to my former wife and to my present wife who, from the very start, have always got on well together, thereby making our children's lives much easier and happier. This advantage has blessed not only the older children but also the younger ones who occasionally visit my former home and enjoy doing so, provided that biscuits are on hand and the dog's kept under control.

At times, the objectivity of the step-parent who is involved, yet not too emotionally involved, can prove quite invaluable. At a time of crisis I well recall when my present wife and my former wife's husband were far wiser about our son, a teenager, than either of us natural parents. Ironically, we parents had to agree with their assessment.

Sadly, far too often, the new partners can take on their partner's old quarrels with a vengeance. If the new partner was involved in the actual break-up then this attitude, although regrettable, is understandable. But if they were not, it is very unfortunate. On remarriage, particularly if both parties remarry, there is a fresh chance of forming a working relationship. So, if the parents are not able to do this, then it is all the more important for a step-parent to try to be a go-between. Sometimes this is out of the question. 'He ran off with her in the first place, how dare she collect David from school?' As time marches on, this attitude can and should soften for the sake of the children, and many a potential court case has been resolved by the quiet help of a discreet step-parent.

In April 1992, Gillian Shephard became Secretary of State for Employment with a seat in the Cabinet. No mean achievement. She is now fifty-two, but when she was thirty-five she married a widower with two children aged eleven and fourteen and gave up her job to look after them. Writing in the *Independent* newspaper she explained how a close friend told her, 'Never forget you can't be their mother, but you can be their very best friend.' What wise advice! 'You can't be their mother but you can be their very best friend.' If only more people realised this there would be much less tension in many a household as more and more people divorce and remarry, bringing their children with them. Mrs Shephard goes on to say, 'I have always treated them as equal and all of them as individuals – rather than extensions of myself as parents often do.' Her stepson, Neil, now twenty-six, shows how well she succeeded. 'My overriding memory of my stepmother is one of fun and humour. There was no threatening scenario because she wasn't a replacement and she never tried to be my mother. She tried deliberately to be my friend. She was always very encouraging . . .'

The difficult child, the difficult partner

What do you do if the stepchild is impossible? This may not happen, but if it does then we have to remember our priorities. Love God, love spouse, love children. Now that you have remarried, after God, your duty is next to love your spouse. Your marriage must come first and always remember that although the difficult child is only on loan to you for a few years, your husband/wife is there for life, or should be. While every effort should be made by both of you to love and cherish the difficult child, in the end your marriage comes first. Some children, even quite young children, quite deliberately and maliciously set out to wreck a new marriage, wishing to keep their parent for themselves. It may take months, even years for a workable harmony or equilibrium to be achieved. Persevere, but in the final analysis your marriage comes first.

Without going back on this at all, it is prudent, particularly in the early years of remarriage, to allow your spouse to have some space in which he can maintain, even develop, his relationship with his own child. Both parent and child need this although, over the years, you may become increasingly part of the scene. Thus, if your husband likes football why not encourage him to take his son to see a football match, just the two of them, while you have an afternoon at home, ending up with a splendid high tea for all three of you? If he were your own son, you might well do this anyway. So there is no need, out of a sense of insecurity, to insist on going too.

We all know of cases where, for no good reason, step-parents have banned children from the home so that either the children have lost all contact with their parent or they have had to continue the relationship in an underhand way. What an indictment of you if your husband can't honestly say, 'I am taking Tom out for a drink this evening,' rather than, 'Sorry I'm late, I had a tough day at the office.' We know one person whose integrity we value considerably. None the less, such is the relationship between his new spouse and the stepchildren, that lies have to be told when these children are seen. 'White lies' are still lies and this surely can't be good for the new marriage.

The wicked step-parent

Nowadays, it is quite usual to find mother with her chil-dren, father with his children (visiting from time to time), coupled with a child or two of the second marriage. Although very hard work, this can be great fun or a total disaster. Much will depend upon your attitude. If there is a golden rule, it surely must be, 'Be fair.' Fiction apart, there are still wicked stepmothers and wicked stepfathers, grossly favouring their own children. This is wrong. Of course, children's demands vary with their age and person-ality and, as parents, we should do our best to meet those demands, at the same time trying to be fair to all. Your one-year-old can bawl more loudly than your thirteen-year-old. Both have needs, albeit different. The baby has an immediate need to be fed or have its nappy changed. Your teenager may need half an hour's undivided atten-tion although she is far too proud or truculent to put this into words. Somehow or other (I often fail) you have to be all things to all children. Joshua (twenty-two) wants to discuss Freud. Emily (twenty) wants to discuss university entrance. Harriet (seven) wants me to admire her painting. Rupert (five) wants to do a puzzle. Benjamin (twelve months) just wants a cuddle. Well, try to be fair!

The family of the step-parent have a role to play although far too few play this role at all generously. However, I was recently encouraged by the story of a man who decided to invite all his grandchildren to spend a holiday with him abroad. One of his children had recently remarried thus gaining two stepchildren. The grandfather insisted on inviting these two children, at his expense, to join this family party about a year or so before he died. Admittedly well-off, he made the gesture which must have reaffirmed and encouraged this new family enormously. Would that this example were followed more often and, I repeat, it is not a question of money. It is a question of concern, encouragement, involvement, of making people feel that they belong.

Making a will

Ending on a sombre note, be fair in life and fair in death. Whatever their ages, your children are still your children. William Shakespeare, by his will, left his wife, Ann Hathaway, 'the second-best bed'. Over 350 years later, I winced on hearing how a middle-aged friend of ours, recently widowed, had been left one dining-room table by her father who had left all his estate to his young daughter in her early twenties. When you die, try to distribute whatever assets you have fairly between your children, making due allowance for any special needs they may have. To my mind, it would not be just to leave everything to your eighteen-year-old son by your second marriage and nothing to your thirty-year-old son by your first marriage. There may be exceptional reasons, but at least start with the principle of equality. Not only is your elder son denied his birthright but, more importantly, he may well feel a sense of bitterness. We should strive to be parents until the day we die. God loves us equally. As parents, in our inner hearts, we may well love our children differently or we may not like them at all equally. All the same, unless there are special circumstances, it should be our duty to treat them equally.

Fiction has not been kind to step-parents, particularly stepmothers. Most of us have been brought up with the story of Cinderella. Her stepmother was bad news as were her stepsisters but, incidentally, why on earth didn't her father do anything about it? Many of us have seen and enjoyed Walt Disney's *Snow White and the Seven Dwarfs*, with its vivid picture of the wicked queen, the stepmother. Fortunately, there are many examples where, for many years, step-parents and stepchildren have enjoyed a rich and rewarding relationship. In rare instances, it can be as rewarding, if not more rewarding, than a normal parent/child relationship because some of the emotional tensions involved in the latter are lacking. Only the pleasure remains. The more you invest in this relationship the better your return.

13 The Role of the Local Church

For more than twenty years Jackie Pullinger has worked among the drug addicts in the walled city in Hong Kong. Her books, *Chasing the Dragon* and *Crack in the Wall* (published by Hodder and Stoughton), make fascinating, inspiring reading. She and her team work among the very poor and disadvantaged, the drug addicts, the drop-outs, the prostitutes, the bottom rung of humanity. Recently, on a short visit to England, she spoke about her ministry with the poor and, among other details, she stressed two principles. First, that every one of us has a direct responsibility to help the poor. In other words, if we pass a beggar in the street, it is our responsibility to go and assist. Of course, the beggar may be a fraud. Our money might be spent on drink or drugs but, be that as it may, we have to do something. We cannot 'pass by on the other side'. Second, she underlined that God created man in his own image and everyone, whatever his or her situation, is entitled to be treated with dignity and with respect. Thus, the smelly beggar in rags is just as valuable to God as the Queen of England. Jackie Pullinger went on to attack the principle of forming a committee before starting to help. In her view, you should help at once and form the committee, if need be, afterwards. In short, you must tackle the immediate problem on your doorstep.

John Wimber of the Vineyard Church, California, makes exactly the same point. He was once taken to task by one of his own congregation who complained that, whereas personally he had done all he could to help a man in trouble, the Church itself had done nothing. To which Wimber replied, 'But you *are* the Church.'

How the Church should behave

The vital point which both these Christian leaders make is that when we are faced with people in trouble, be it divorce or any other problem, we should help them ourselves. We should never underestimate our personal contribution. Thereafter, we may find that the problem is too big for us to handle alone and we may have to involve others, perhaps even the professionals. Yet, at the point of crisis, we must stand in the gap. Furthermore, we should always remember that we may well be the only Christians that they know. They may have come to us quite by chance or because they know that we are Christians. Either way, how we react initially may well colour their view of us (which matters very little) but also their view of Christ (which matters enormously). It may well have cost them a good deal to seek our help in the first place and we must be prepared to read between the lines. Children are sometimes difficult to reach when they have something on their minds. You have to probe gently to find out what is really worrying them: adults are just the same.

On this point, I recall visiting a doctor many years ago for an apparently trivial problem. If he had had any pastoral skill or concern at all, he should have realised that there was something far more important to discuss. He either couldn't or wouldn't see beyond a trivial request and he merely wrote out a prescription and sent for the next patient.

We should be sensitive, trusting our gut instinct when people approach us for help. We may have to help them unburden themselves.

Thus, our immediate reaction is all-important. We may be very busy, very tired or just plain out of our depth but, whatever the circumstances, we must respond practically and lovingly and read between the lines.

Your neighbour comes round in floods of tears because she has found a letter in her husband's pocket. Your workmate suddenly asks you out for a drink, which he has never done before. If at all possible, respond. Your immediate help may seem very trivial but could make all the difference. If a person comes to you in distress, then give them a seat, have a handkerchief to hand, listen and put on the kettle. Thereafter, you may have to call in reinforcements, but just consider how you would feel if, with a roaring toothache, your dentist told you to book an appointment for Tuesday week.

Divorce recovery teams and seminars

Once this personal link has been established, then clearly the local church has a considerable role to play and, depending on the make-up of your church, in both numbers and character, you are far more suited to decide the details than I am. The following suggestions as to how to build up a divorce recovery team and have seminars are therefore made with some diffidence. They have been evolved, by trial and error, over many months, so adapt them as you will. We are still learning all the time.

The blessing of the minister

If this ministry of helping others is going to be conducted under the aegis of the local church and particularly on church premises, it is immeasurably strengthened if the minister gives it his general blessing. We are all under the authority of God and our minister's authority should be respected. If he can give a general endorsement to our ministry, always provided that he approves of it, it helps to give us a status. Status itself matters very little but, particularly where raw emotions are involved, it could well be dangerous if such a ministry were quite independent of your church. The minister need not fear that, by encouraging you, he is condoning divorce. Far from it. As this book makes clear, every effort should be made to uphold and improve marriage.

However, if the marriage fails, despite all these efforts, surely we can all rally round and help the wounded, particularly the children, to the best of our ability? To give a simple analogy. We may not approve of excessive drinking. Does this mean that we do not help the man crippled with cirrhosis of the liver or his wife or his children? Again, we may not approve of smoking. If lung cancer follows, do we ignore his needs and those of his family? Once the minister has given his general blessing and encouragement, he may well decide to take a low profile. It is probably better for him to do so since, with rare exceptions, his personal experience may well be very limited. I hope it is. Pastorally he will know all about it but he will not have been through it.

Building a team

Teams choose themselves. When our divorce seminars started, we were greatly helped by people whom we barely knew who courageously and generously volunteered to help. They were not necessarily the people we had even considered at all. Yet, years later, they still remain stalwart helpers. It's as well to start small. It is amazing how a good idea, if blessed by God, spreads like a bush fire. You will probably find that the majority of your helpers have themselves been divorced or have had intimate family experience of divorce. The present Archbishop of Canterbury, George Carey, has a divorced daughter and has publicly acknowledged the lessons that this has taught him. Single people, whether widowed or unmarried, may well have valuable contributions to make. The broader the mix of age and background the better.

Train the team

On one view, training is essential. On another, experience, particularly Christian experience and the ability to listen and learn, constantly guided by the Holy Spirit, are sufficient. Since these problems are often so deep and difficult, it is a great help if at least some of the team have had experience in general counselling. This need not be divorce counselling. Just as pain cannot be put into compartments, neither can human problems. 'There is no hierarchy of horrors,' as someone said. Very often, the person involved in a divorce has other problems as well. So the wider the experience of the team the better. Putting the matter at its very lowest, all the team should be sufficiently experienced to know when they are out of their depth and the team leader should be able to assist, gently and tactfully, in guiding the victim to suitable helpers.

Building up a team spirit

'Team spirit' has a schoolboy ring about it. Yet, the better the team know themselves the more effective they will be as a team. We all find out our strengths and weaknesses in community and, if we are going to be effective as helpers, we must ourselves be prepared to put ourselves on the line. It is not, repeat not, a 'we' and 'them' situation. In many senses, we are all victims and we are all helpers so we must be frank and open with each other, as a team, before we start ministering to others. Furthermore, as a team, we may well want to discuss certain problems which we ourselves are finding difficult to handle. If we do this, we must always remember confidentiality. In a large church such as ours, this may not be such a problem because it is quite possible to discuss a problem in such general terms that the person concerned cannot be identified. In smaller churches, this is very much harder to achieve. There are only three publicans in your church. Fred is on holiday. John is in hospital so the person you are discussing must be William. Take great care to respect confidentiality. At the same time, if you have a difficult problem, provided you either have the person's permission or can suitably disguise who that person is, share the problem with your team.

A word of warning: it is not unknown for an unsuitable person to join the team. Their unsuitability may well not become apparent at first glance and they may well be properly trained or give the appearance of being properly trained. It is only when meeting them informally, perhaps on a picnic or in a pub, that you realise that they are quite unsuitable. This is a knotty problem. If they cannot be neutralised or shunted sideways to another type of ministry, you may well have to ask your minister to intervene. Yours is a difficult and delicate ministry and you cannot afford to hurt people who are hurt enough anyway. Let's hope you do not have this problem, but I fear you may.

List of experts

Have a list of experts to hand. This list should be constantly kept up to date. Preferably, these experts should be known personally by one of you or by someone you respect. Remember that partnerships and firms of solicitors and accountants often change. It is not good enough just to recommend 'Whinge and Whine' because Mr Whinge may have retired and Miss Whine (now young Mrs Whinge) may be having a baby. There is a danger in being too specific in your recommendations because, first of all, you are putting your own reputation at stake and, second, it could well be said that, like the freemasons, you are seeking to keep work within the fraternity. Being Christian is no guarantee of competence. If the best child psychiatrist you know is an agnostic, recommend him. You can always point out his or her beliefs when doing so. This list, although constantly revised, should be unofficial, almost unwritten. I would not recommend merely handing out a list of names and addresses. Far better to have a chat with the person concerned and say something on the lines of, 'Well, look, I could be wrong but I think that either Dr X or Dr Y are the best and why not contact AA at the same time. Here are the addresses.'

Books and tapes

Suitable books and tapes are essential, as has already been discussed. Only recommend them if you have mastered them yourself unless you give an honest disclaimer. For example, I have not read all James Dobson's books but, without hesitation, I would recommend you to read any of them. Try and keep these books and tapes up to date. When I became a Christian in 1980, such writers as David Watson and Catherine Marshall were very much in vogue. Thirteen years later, other writers may well have super-seded them, at least in certain topics. We all of us tend to get trapped in our own generation's thinking, despite the dismal evidence of the mirror, that we are still with it and up to date.

Some years ago, the well-known Christian children's songwriter and singer, Ishmael, spoke at our church. Amusingly, he teased us about our music, saying that although we considered it was modern it was in fact mainly the music of the 1960s, in short, sanctified Beatle music. The same applies with books and tapes. If you are in your fifties and want to give someone in their twenties a suitable book on marriage, it may be as well to ask your younger friends what they would advise. God's truth never alters. Classic Christian books will undoubtedly stand the test of time but up-to-date presentation may well meet the need of the moment. The King James version of the Bible is beautiful but, for the new convert, many might rec-ommend more modern translations. Finally, have an eye to how these books are designed. Far too many Christian books still have soppy covers even if the contents are worth reading. Paperbacks are probably a better bet than hardbacks and are easier to give away both because they are cheaper and because they do not put the recipient under so much of a sense of obligation. Always have these books and tapes attractively displayed.

A suitable room

If possible, find a suitable room. People coming to such seminars are vulnerable. They have probably come with considerable misgivings, carrying many burdens. What is more, if they have young children it has probably been both hard and expensive for them to get a babysitter. Make them welcome. A largish room in a private house or an attractively carpeted small room off the church is far better than bare boards and draughty windows. The tea should be hot, the sandwiches fresh and the biscuits edible. The room should be attractive and so should you! Our mission is to build up people, to restore and encourage them, making them realise that, with God's help, there is light at the end of the tunnel.

Years ago, I worked for a High Court judge, the Rt Hon. Mr Justice Stable, MC. He was splendid, full of compassion and common sense. I always remember a story he told of an attractive young prostitute who came before him for serious offences of dishonesty. He was minded to put her on probation and sent for the probation officer. This probation officer was grim and dowdy with a sour judgmental face. As the old judge put it, 'My boy, how could I get it across to this young woman that vice didn't pay and virtue did? I fined her instead.'

At all costs, we should avoid being judgmental. We helpers should always remember that we ourselves are in need of help. All of us sin. All of us are vulnerable and have made and will make many mistakes in life. The line between helper and victim is very fine. The more you give the more you get. I learn this from every seminar I give, from every book I read and from every person I meet. So, be open. Be natural, be honest and, above all, be loving.

14 Divorce Recovery Seminars – a suggested outline

At Holy Trinity, Brompton, we have been running divorce recovery seminars for some time. We have the advantage of being members of a large church in central London with good facilities, pleasant rooms and able and devoted staff, both ordained and lay. On the other hand, there are drawbacks with so large a church, not least that people can get lost and lonely and we sometimes find that we do not know all the helpers, let alone the victims, quite a few of whom come from other churches.

How you run your groups or seminars is entirely your affair. Much will depend on the size of your church, how many people are available and many other factors. You are just as much a helper talking to one distressed person in your kitchen as running a divorce recovery seminar in the Albert Hall. We are all labourers in God's vineyard, of equal value to him, whether we help gather one grape or a thousand.

Since we hold these seminars in the converted crypt of the church and all of us are committed Christians, we make our religious convictions clear throughout but we are delighted, really delighted, when people come to us who are outside the Christian fold. We earnestly wish to help anyone and everyone and all of us try very hard not to be 'churchy' or 'religious'. We considered whether we might help more people outside the church if we were less overtly Christian. Undoubtedly, such organisations as Relate (formerly Marriage Guidance) who specialise in counselling, with no religious input, do an invaluable job.

It is entirely up to you and you may well decide to tone down your religious convictions, depending on your audience.

Although many of the practical points are useful, whatever the person's religious belief, I am quite sure that it is better to be bold because God, by his Holy Spirit, can work wonders, whereas mere human advice is just that. If people can be brought into a living relationship with Jesus Christ then, although their problems will not disappear overnight, they are essentially well on the road to recovery. Our outreach here is not directly evangelistic. In other words, there is not a direct effort to bring people into the kingdom of God but underlying all is our compassionate conviction that Jesus is the way, the truth and the life.

Running a series

We hold seminars twice a year, in spring and autumn, meeting on five consecutive Monday evenings. The need is so urgent that an annual course would not be sufficient and, at the moment, we do not have the time or energy to run more than two a year. What about the intervening period? After our first seminar, quite a few of us felt that we had deserted some of the people who came. This is because, after weeks of rather intense relationships, the seminars ended and we all went home leaving them high and dry. This worried us. Our present solution is two-fold. First, some of us, via the church, are always available informally. Second, by letter, we try to keep in loose touch and suggest that there are fortnightly fellowship meetings which people may care to join. The particular fellowship we recommend is not an exclusive divorce group, but it does contain leaders who have themselves been divorced. We have found that these two methods help keep people afloat in the intervening months.

Some years ago, at our church, a group was started by a converted homosexual to help homosexuals, many of whom live in the Earls Court area of London where the church helps the Earls Court Project, an outreach to the drug addicts, homosexuals and homeless in that area. The church leaders rightly endorsed this group but stressed that it should try very hard not to be just for homosexuals.

We take exactly the same view about the divorced. One of the limitations of modern life is that the race relations industry, for example, always sees all problems in race relations terms. Socialist politicians, Conservative politicians are the same, always seeing in Socialist or Conservative terms. The Christian family, all of us brothers and sisters in a personal relationship with Jesus Christ, is quite different. We are not just black or white, rich or poor, divorced or married. We are many faceted, with much potential, if only we will let God rule our lives. Therefore, as far as we possibly can, we always encourage those we meet through our divorce ministry to put it behind them and join enthusiastically the wider world and the wider church.

Throughout the year our church, like many others, runs various courses. It has an excellent course on Christian basics called the Alpha course. Quite a few have gone from our seminars on to some of these courses and, only a few Sundays ago, I was immensely encouraged when an attractive, vibrant woman, who had been far less so when she started with us, gave her testimony in church. She had joined an Alpha course, gone away for a weekend houseparty with a very mixed bunch of Christians and, wholeheartedly, had joined the church fellowship. God has given us all many talents and gifts and we should strive to use them all. So we are delighted when people move on, out of the divorce ghetto.

Returning to our seminar series, although people are free to come and go over the five weeks, we try to encourage people to attend all five evenings. People who are tentatively forming some rapport with a helper are naturally disappointed when that helper does not turn up the following week. It takes time for relationships to form and for a sense of fellowship to develop, but we always welcome anyone who wants to come and, particularly with people whose family commitments make regular attendance difficult, always stress that we can catch up on the details at another time.

I am always amazed, facing the audience on the first night, by how much the same audience have relaxed by the last night. Time and time again, the most unlikely people have struck up a friendship although, on occasions, we have made specific introductions. Beware of typecasting people. You may have an army officer as a helper and an out-of-work labourer as a victim. In human terms, they have very little in common but since both their wives committed adultery, you may well find that they speak the same language. Likewise, as any family support group for Alcoholics Anonymous will confirm, two women dealing with alcoholic husbands have very much in common. Let them find each other out if you can although, on occasions, you may have to break the ice on the lines of, 'Alice, do meet Jane – she knows only too much about violence.'

Throughout, we always try to remember that we are all in this together. In a sense, we are all helpers, we are all victims.

A suggested timetable

This timetable has evolved from trial and error. We may well alter it again and, no doubt, you will have different ideas.

6.30 p.m.   Helpers meet to pray, both generally and specifically, and to discuss problems. These may have arisen from the last seminar or have come up during the week. Confidentiality can present difficulties but, in so large a church, it is easier to be anonymous, at least for a while. We meet discreetly in a separate room from the seminar room, leaving coffee and biscuits outside the seminar room.

7.30 p.m.   Short notes being provided, I give a talk lasting approximately one hour. The idea is not to speak *at* the group but rather to share *with* the group. Questions are not encouraged at this stage; the material to get through is quite extensive.

8.30 p.m.   Coffee, with biscuits, sandwiches and fruit. We provide this, thanks to some stalwart helpers, and we consider this coffee break most important, enabling us all to meet and chat informally. It is scheduled for half an hour but often continues for three-quarters of an hour. On the fifth evening, with warning, we have more of a party, with food and drink.

9.00 p.m.   We go back to the seminar room for
(approx.)   open discussion, ending with prayer. This part of the evening is always a venture into the unknown. How will the Holy Spirit take us? So far, we have discovered that, for the first one or two seminars, whereas the discussion is frank and open, the prayer is usually rather formal and tentative. Rather than frighten people whose vulnerability and dignity must always be respected, we sometimes end the open meeting quite early, allowing them to escape, then reforming into smaller groups, as people want and as the Spirit moves.

9.30–10.00 p.m.   Departure, people being free to go whenever they like. We try to make it as easy for people to leave as to come. Babysitters can be a hassle. We end formally at 10.00 p.m. although some of us leave later.

If you wish to order the set of five tapes, with an accompanying booklet, please contact The Vestry, Holy Trinity, Brompton, Brompton Road, London SW7 1JA. Telephone: 071-581 8255.

Postscript

Why me?

A final word of encouragement to all enmeshed in divorce.

'Why me?' I well remember asking that question, 'Why me?'

Why does God allow some of us to go through such hell?

My conclusions are most tentative but, for what they are worth, the following may be of some assistance. First, all of us have to accept that, to some extent at least, we are to blame. In any marriage breakdown, it is never 100 per cent the other person's fault. Therefore, to the extent of our blame, as Christians, we must repent, seek God's forgiveness and receive his forgiveness. We cannot deal with our partner's sins but we can, at the very least, deal with our own. Second, we all live in a fallen world although we know that in the end God will prevail. In this fallen world, sin is often triumphant and thus, indirectly if not directly, we are afflicted by it and our marriages thereby undermined, perhaps destroyed. Third, many events in life are quite inexplicable. Why should your baby die of a cot death? Why should your sister die of cancer, leaving a husband and three young children? There is no complete answer and it would be futile to attempt one.

BUT, 'We know that in everything God works for good with those who love him, who are called according to his purpose' (Rom. 8:28). God does not make mistakes and with the help of the Holy Spirit you can emerge stronger rather than weaker from this experience.

Over twenty-three years ago, my first son, Harry, died after only thirty-six hours. At the time, his death seemed monstrously unfair and, in one sense, it undoubtedly was.

Now, with hindsight, I am quite certain his death was one of the best things that has ever happened to me in that it began the process of breaking me down so that, with God's grace, I could begin to understand how other people felt and how other people suffered. Your suffering can do the same for you. It can make you or mar you.

May I end with the prayer Moses taught to Aaron, to be found in Numbers 6:24–6:

> The Lord bless you and keep you:
> The Lord make his face to shine upon you,
>   and be gracious to you:
> The Lord lift up his countenance upon you,
>   and give you peace.

Chiswick, 1993

Book List

I would recommend *any* book by Dr James Dobson

Marriage Alive, Richard and Joyce Conner (Diasozo Trust, 1986)

Marriage On The Mend, Joyce Huggett (Kingsway, 1987)

Intended For Pleasure, Ed and Gaye Wheat (Scripture Union, 1979)

Christian Marriage, Helen Lee (Mowbrays, 1977)

Pressure Points, Peter Meadows (Kingsway, 1988)

Divorce – The Forgivable Sin?, Ken Crispin (Hodder and Stoughton, 1989)

What Teenagers Can Tell Us About Divorce And Step-families, Julia Tugendhat (Bloomsbury, 1990)

How Can I Forgive?, Vera Sinton (Lion, 1990)

Divorced Christians And The Love Of God, Paula Clifford (Triangle, 1987)

The Which Guide To Divorce, Helen Garlick (Hodder and Stoughton, 1992)